New D

C000177647

Edited by **Sally Welch**   May–August 2022

15 The Chambers, Vineyard
Abingdon OX14 3FE
brf.org.uk

Bible Reading Fellowship is a charity (233280)
and company limited by guarantee (301324),
registered in England and Wales

ISBN 978 1 80039 084 3
All rights reserved

This edition © Bible Reading Fellowship 2022
Cover image © scalige/stock.adobe.com

Distributed in Australia by:
MediaCom Education Inc, PO Box 610, Unley, SA 5061
Tel: 1 800 811 311 | admin@mediacom.org.au

Distributed in New Zealand by:
Scripture Union Wholesale, PO Box 760, Wellington 6140
Tel: 04 385 0421 | suwholesale@clear.net.nz

Acknowledgements
Scripture quotations marked with the following abbreviations are taken from
the version shown. **NIV:** The Holy Bible, New International Version, Anglicised
edition, copyright © 1979, 1984, 2011 by Biblica. Used by permission of Hodder
& Stoughton Publishers, an Hachette UK company. All rights reserved. 'NIV' is a
registered trademark of Biblica. UK trademark number 1448790. **NRSV:** The New
Revised Standard Version of the Bible, Anglicised Edition, copyright © 1989, 1995
by the Division of Christian Education of the National Council of the Churches
of Christ in the USA. Used by permission. All rights reserved. **MSG:** The Message,
copyright © 1993, 1994, 1995, 1996, 2000, 2001, 2002 by Eugene H. Peterson. Used
by permission of NavPress. All rights reserved. Represented by Tyndale House
Publishers, Inc. **ISV:** The Holy Bible: International Standard Version. Release 2.0,
Build 2015.02.09. Copyright © 1995–2014 by ISV Foundation. All rights reserved
internationally. Used by permission of Davidson Press, LLC. **WEB:** The World
English Bible. Public Domain. **ESV:** The Holy Bible, English Standard Version,
published by HarperCollins Publishers, © 2001 Crossway Bibles, a division of Good
News Publishers. Used by permission. All rights reserved.

A catalogue record for this book is available from the British Library

Printed by Gutenberg Press, Tarxien, Malta

Suggestions for using *New Daylight*

Find a regular time and place, if possible, where you can read and pray undisturbed. Before you begin, take time to be still and perhaps use one of the BRF prayers on page 6. Then read the Bible passage slowly (try reading it aloud if you find it over-familiar), followed by the comment. You can also use *New Daylight* for group study and discussion, if you prefer.

The prayer or point for reflection can be a starting point for your own meditation and prayer. Many people like to keep a journal to record their thoughts about a Bible passage and items for prayer. In *New Daylight* we also note the Sundays and some special festivals from the church calendar, to keep in step with the Christian year.

New Daylight and the Bible

New Daylight contributors use a range of Bible versions, and you will find a list of the versions used opposite. You are welcome to use your own preferred version alongside the passage printed in the notes. This can be particularly helpful if the Bible text has been abridged.

New Daylight affirms that the whole of the Bible is God's revelation to us, and we should read, reflect on and learn from every part of both Old and New Testaments. Usually the printed comment presents a straightforward 'thought for the day', but sometimes it may also raise questions rather than simply providing answers, as we wrestle with some of the more difficult passages of scripture.

New Daylight is also available in a deluxe edition (larger format). Visit your local Christian bookshop or **brfonline.org.uk**. To obtain an audio version for the blind or partially sighted, contact Torch Trust for the Blind, Torch House, Torch Way, Northampton Road, Market Harborough LE16 9HL; +44 (0)1858 438260; **info@torchtrust.org**.

Comment on *New Daylight*

To send feedback, please email **enquiries@brf.org.uk**, phone **+44 (0)1865 319700** or write to the address shown opposite.

Writers in this issue

Louise Davis is part of the team at the Arthur Rank Centre, the national organisation for the rural church, where she runs a leadership development programme and edits *Country Way* magazine. In her spare time, Louise is the volunteer chaplain to Leicester City Women Football Club.

Murdo Macdonald is a molecular biologist, with over 20 years experience working in research labs, including almost a decade serving with the Leprosy Mission in Nepal. Since 2008 Murdo has led the Society, Religion and Technology Project of the Church of Scotland.

Bob Mayo is the Anglican prison chaplain at HMP Wormwood Scrubs.

Lucy Moore is the founder and pioneer of Messy Church. Her writing over recent years has been almost exclusively Messy Church-related. She is currently working with local teams to set up new Messy Churches in the Peak District.

Elizabeth Rundle has written many study and devotional books including *20 Questions Jesus Asked* for BRF. She has written and presented scripts for local and national radio and television, and organised and led 16 pilgrimages to the Holy Land.

Andrea Skevington is a writer, speaker and blogger from Suffolk. Her writings include an award-winning retelling of the Bible, and her poetry has featured on Radio 3's *The Verb*. She is drawn to Celtic Christianity and the natural world. *Jesus Said, 'I Am'* is her latest book for BRF.

Naomi Starkey is a priest in the Church in Wales, based in a group of North Anglesey churches and also working more widely as a pioneer evangelist.

Sheila Walker has been a teacher, editor, single parent, author, information officer, grandmother and is currently serving as associate minister with three rural churches. She enjoys words, walking and holidays in Wales.

Veronica Zundel is an Oxford graduate, writer and columnist. She lives with her husband and son in North London. Her most recent book is *Everything I Know about God, I've Learned from Being a Parent* (BRF, 2013).

Sally Welch writes…

I have been the editor of *New Daylight* since 2016. I have commissioned and edited 20 issues, trying to meet the challenge of producing Bible reading notes which are relevant, interesting, challenging, supportive and encouraging. Above all, my aim has been to share the good news of the gospel in a way which deepens our relationship with Jesus Christ. I have been helped and supported in this aim by a wonderful team of writers, and I am profoundly grateful for their contributions. I have also been both challenged and supported by the many letters I have received from readers, some of whom have become regular correspondents. Whenever I commission a new writer, I remind them that our first priority is you, the reader, and that whatever we write should be done with you in mind, and I hope that I have been successful in communicating this to you.

As much as I have enjoyed this work, it is now time to hand over the task. I do so reluctantly, but knowing it is the right thing both for me and, more importantly, for *New Daylight*. The new editor is Gordon Giles, canon chancellor of Rochester Cathedral. He is an excellent choice, and I am sure that *New Daylight* will be in good hands with him. I will continue to contribute as a writer, sharing the journey as we go forwards.

This issue begins with my writing on 'Standing still', continuing with our theme for this year: 'Look back and remember, he was with you; stand still and realise, he is with you; walk forward and trust, he will be with you always.' I share with you my reflections on the habit of Christian mindfulness – being aware of Christ in the present moment and celebrating his love. I end with a favourite quote of mine: 'Let this presence settle into your bones, and allow your soul the freedom to sing, dance, praise and love' (Teresa of Ávila).

It is my prayer that the reflections in *New Daylight* have enabled God's presence to 'settle into your bones' and helped your soul to freedom and that they will continue to do so.

Sally Ann Welch

The BRF Prayer

Almighty God,
you have taught us that your word is a lamp for our feet
and a light for our path. Help us, and all who prayerfully
read your word, to deepen our fellowship with you
and with each other through your love.
And in so doing may we come to know you more fully,
love you more truly, and follow more faithfully
in the steps of your Son Jesus Christ, who lives and reigns
with you and the Holy Spirit, one God forevermore.
Amen

The BRF Centenary Prayer

Gracious God,
we rejoice in this centenary year
that you have grown BRF
from a local network of Bible readers
into a worldwide family of ministries.
Thank you for your faithfulness
in nurturing small beginnings
into surprising blessings.
We rejoice that, from the youngest to the oldest,
so many have encountered your word
and grown as disciples of Christ.
Keep us humble in your service,
ambitious for your glory
and open to new opportunities.
For your name's sake
Amen

Standing still

Some years ago I attended an introductory course on mind-fulness – the practice of paying attention to the world as it is without judgement, simply appreciating the moment and allowing ourselves to rest in it, undistracted by memory or anticipation and fully engaged with the present. It was an excellent course, encouraging me to step off the merry-go-round of internal commentary, anxious expectation and regretful nostalgia and simply witness what was happening at the time. I learnt how to receive with gratitude the experiences which the present offered and to give myself space to think and feel differently, without being tied to past behaviours or future plans. I was invited to adopt a compassionate outlook on life and to be patient with my own faults, enabling me to look kindly on others.

The course, however, was designed for secular use, and to me it seemed hollow. Secular mindfulness, I felt, brought me to the moment of realising God's love for me without inviting me to accept it, the moment of appreciating creation without acknowledging the creator. Christian mindfulness, the practice of 'standing still' and realising that God is with us all, all the time, enables us to honour God within us and thus honour God beyond us.

Mindful prayer teaches us to begin where we are and to journey on from there in the company of Christ, who is both our guide and our destination. We learn to have faith in God's love and to rest in the security of the cross, knowing we are forgiven and redeemed. From that place of security, we can reach out to others in service and love, free from judging or condemning because we are ourselves no longer judged but simply loved.

The Bible is full of moments of stillness, of invitations to rest in the presence of God, listening for his voice in the silence, aware of his love surrounding us. Even in the busiest of times, this stillness can be ours, as we focus on the 'now', which is where we will find him. As Ignatius Loyola said, 'Those who carry God in their hearts, bear heaven with them wherever they go.'

SALLY WELCH

Step aside

Now Moses was tending the flock of Jethro his father-in-law, the priest of Midian, and he led the flock to the far side of the wilderness and came to Horeb, the mountain of God. There the angel of the Lord appeared to him in flames of fire from within a bush. Moses saw that though the bush was on fire it did not burn up. So Moses thought, 'I will go over and see this strange sight – why the bush does not burn up.' When the Lord saw that he had gone over to look, God called to him from within the bush, 'Moses! Moses!' And Moses said, 'Here I am.'

I once accompanied my father on a business trip to the United States. Driving hundreds of miles from one conference to the next in a large, air-conditioned van with comfortable seating, I was content to sit and watch the scenery unfold before my eyes. My father, however, insisted on stopping at almost every 'site of interest' – even though I was not interested at all. Out we would get, to stand one foot either side of a state line, or gaze at a geological feature, or wander round a historic building which was newer than my house. But each time we stopped, we learned something. Each time we appreciated more the bewildering variety of features which make up the US. Each time I climbed back in the car, I was glad I had got out.

Moses' encounter with God in the wilderness is a direct result of him stepping off the beaten track, taking just a few steps away from his daily routine of leading a flock of sheep from one grazing place to another. God has a mission for Moses, but he cannot communicate that mission unless Moses stops to listen. Only when Moses gets near enough can he hear the call and respond.

Sometimes we need to step aside from our daily routine, or at least not let ourselves become so numbed to it that we are oblivious to the wonders that surround us each day. It is only when we are listening that we stand any chance of hearing.

Lord, help me to hear your call for me.

SALLY WELCH

Wanting and needing

The Lord is my shepherd, I shall not want. He makes me lie down in green pastures; he leads me beside still waters; he restores my soul.

We live in a world which seeks to maintain a sense of scarcity in us. We are far more aware of what we don't have than what we do, because if we don't have it, we are more likely to go out and try to buy it, thus supporting our consumer economy.

But this, by definition, does not lead to satisfaction. So often the more we have, the more we want. We are consumed by what we consume – filled with images of what we desire instead of recognising what we already have; driven to get more instead of celebrating what we have; measuring ourselves against who we are not, rather than rejoicing in who we are.

Psalm 23 is a radical reminder of the sufficiency of God and an encouragement to believe in that sufficiency. It is also an encouragement to pause and reflect on the things – both material and spiritual – that we want in our lives. Are they different from the things we really need? These first verses encourage us to take time to consider the landscape of our hearts and souls. Do we spend too much time thinking of ourselves and our needs, and pay little regard to those with whom we share our lives? Or have we served others to such an extent that our own lives have become empty and in need of refreshment?

In either case, it is God to whom we must turn for restoration and refreshment. It is he who will help us to reflect on our priorities; he who will show us the places where we can rest and relax, by still waters and in green pastures. But these are only temporary resting places, and we must not be deluded that our pausing place is our stopping place. The psalmist, like us, is on a journey and is continuously on the move until he reaches his destination.

Lord God, help me to follow where you lead,
trusting in the sufficiency of your love for me.

SALLY WELCH

Silence

For God alone my soul waits in silence; from him comes my salvation. He alone is my rock and my salvation, my fortress; I shall never be shaken… For God alone my soul waits in silence, for my hope is from him. He alone is my rock and my salvation, my fortress; I shall not be shaken. On God rests my deliverance and my honour; my mighty rock, my refuge is in God. Trust in him at all times, O people; pour out your heart before him; God is a refuge for us.

Our lives today are too often filled with noise – from the reassuring background noise of radio or television, which reminds us that we are not alone on the planet, to our favourite songs transmitted to us through headphones while we exercise, to music carefully designed to encourage us to eat quicker or spend more when we are in restaurants or shops. That is above the noise we make – our conversations with other people or the endless dialogue which takes place in our own heads, providing a constant commentary on our thoughts and actions.

Silence can seem threatening and frightening. It can force us to examine our own thoughts and motives; it can bring to the front of our minds things which we prefer to hide. But silence is vital for our souls' well-being. In its depths we can seek stillness, allowing our soul to wait on God. It is in this stillness, this sacred rest, that our souls can be restored as the endless noise of activity which surrounds us is paused and we make space to hear the still small voice of God. It doesn't need to be an extended period of time, certainly not to begin with, and it might help to have a timer set for three or four minutes, just to engage with silence, and allow God's voice to be heard.

Breathe through the heats of our desire
your coolness and your balm;
let sense be dumb, let flesh retire,
speak through the earthquake, wind and fire,
O still small voice of calm,
O still small voice of calm.
(John Greenleaf Whittier, 1807–92)

SALLY WELCH

Considering lilies

'Therefore I tell you, do not worry about your life, what you will eat or what you will drink, or about your body, what you will wear. Is not life more than food, and the body more than clothing? Look at the birds of the air; they neither sow nor reap nor gather into barns, and yet your heavenly Father feeds them. Are you not of more value than they? And can any of you by worrying add a single hour to your span of life? And why do you worry about clothing? Consider the lilies of the field, how they grow; they neither toil nor spin, yet I tell you, even Solomon in all his glory was not clothed like one of these.'

One of my favourite quotations comes from Alice Walker's novel *The Color Purple* (1982). In it she describes a sensation of connectedness with the whole of creation: 'That feeling of being part of everything, not separate at all. I knew that if I cut a tree, my arm would bleed.' She goes on to write, 'I think it pisses God off if you walk by the color purple in a field somewhere and don't notice it.'

Jesus invites us to 'consider the lilies of the field' – and it can be a useful exercise to do just that. It doesn't have to be a lily; any object found in nature will do, whether a pine cone, a flower, a stick or a leaf. We can spend time simply appreciating it for what it is, noticing its detail, delighting in its strength and its frailty, reflecting on its place within the order of creation.

That something so tiny and to all appearances insignificant can have such care lavished on its design and construction serves to remind us how gloriously we ourselves are made, in the image of God.

To see a World in a Grain of Sand
And a Heaven in a Wild Flower
Hold Infinity in the palm of your hand
And Eternity in an hour.
('Auguries of Innocence' by William Blake)

SALLY WELCH

A moment of stillness

The teachers of the law and the Pharisees brought in a woman caught in adultery. They made her stand before the group and said to Jesus, 'Teacher, this woman was caught in the act of adultery. In the Law Moses commanded us to stone such women. Now what do you say?' They were using this question as a trap, in order to have a basis for accusing him. But Jesus bent down and started to write on the ground with his finger. When they kept on questioning him, he straightened up and said to them, 'Let any one of you who is without sin be the first to throw a stone at her.' Again he stooped down and wrote on the ground. At this, those who heard began to go away one at a time, the older ones first, until only Jesus was left, with the woman still standing there.

What a heated moment this is! Jesus' enemies are determined to trap him and will stoop to any level to do so. The means they have at hand is not a trick question or a hypothetical example, but a human being. She is only a woman, they might have argued. She was worth little anyway and has further degraded herself by adultery. She is dispensable.

They must have crowded round Jesus, holding before them the poor, shamed woman, trembling and frightened for her life. They hoped to catch Jesus out, so that they could condemn him and get rid of him.

But Jesus doesn't respond as expected. Instead he turns the questioning away from him to them. He holds up a mirror to their actions, then steps back and allows them to look at their own reflections. Appalled by what they see, the woman's accusers steal away, until only she is left.

It can take great courage to gaze at our soul's reflection in the mirror of Christ. Undoubtedly, we will not like what we see. But if we continue to gaze, in sorrow and repentance, we will see another figure besides that of ourselves – that of Jesus himself, on the cross, holding out his arms in forgiveness and love.

'Go now and leave your life of sin' (John 8:11).

SALLY WELCH

The touch of love

The evening meal was in progress, and the devil had already prompted Judas, the son of Simon Iscariot, to betray Jesus. Jesus knew that the Father had put all things under his power, and that he had come from God and was returning to God; so he got up from the meal, took off his outer clothing, and wrapped a towel around his waist. After that, he poured water into a basin and began to wash his disciples' feet, drying them with the towel that was wrapped round him.

Feet are not in themselves terribly attractive objects – and I suspect the disciples' feet were less attractive than most. Leather sandals were the only protection against the onslaught of stones, thorns, dust and heat. Patches of hard skin would develop from where straps had rubbed, and there would be scabs and sores from insect bites and grazes and scrapes from stumbles or climbs. The smell of old leather would rub off on feet already ripe with sweat and the dirt of animal waste and dust. These were the feet that Jesus washed. These were the feet that he cradled tenderly in his hands, wiping away the stains of travel, drying them carefully before releasing them, cleansed and renewed.

So, too, Jesus takes our hearts and souls, weary from the trials of the world, the conflict and the sorrow, the pain and the hurt. He heals them with his love, bathes them in the water of life, and sets us again to face the world, refreshed and restored.

And we can do the same in our turn, as we greet those around us with joy and love, as we serve our community in ways which bring healing and wholeness, as we build up ourselves and each other in the body of Christ.

Not every act of service is pleasant, and very often they are ungraciously received or even despised. But still we kneel beside the souls of those with whom we share our lives, offering love in the name of the one who first loved us.

'Not all of us can do great things. But we can do small things with great love' (attributed to Mother Teresa of Calcutta).

SALLY WELCH

Now is the time

See what love the Father has given us, that we should be called children of God; and that is what we are. The reason the world does not know us is that it did not know him. Beloved, we are God's children now; what we will be has not yet been revealed. What we do know is this: when he is revealed, we will be like him, for we will see him as he is.

The first letter of John is a letter of love. Infused with love for God in Christ, and the living out of that love through service to fellow Christians and beyond, John repeats again and again his belief in the power of God's love. It drops like water on a stone, gradually eroding the hard places, smoothing away the roughness and the angularity, until the stone is polished and round, reflecting light from its entire surface.

If ever there was a call to begin a new way of living, this is it. If ever there was a challenge to set aside our hurts and our grievances, to move past the obstacles that have been placed in the way of our relationship with God – placed by us or by others, by circumstance or by unwise decisions – this is it. If ever there was a time to begin again, it is now. 'We are God's children now,' declares John. We don't have to wait until everything is in order. We don't have to wait until we are in the right frame of mind. We just have to begin and live – live in the moment; live as those who are loved deeply and completely; live rejoicing in each minute of God's company, which we can enjoy from now until eternity.

There is huge potential within each one of us, potential for becoming more fully the person God intended us to be. We do not know how that potential will be realised, nor what part we will play in the salvation of creation, but we do all have a part. Let us begin to play it, with all our hearts.

'Let this presence settle into your bones, and allow your soul the freedom to sing, dance, praise and love' (Teresa of Ávila).

SALLY WELCH

Celebration

'When Jesus had called the Twelve together, he gave them power and authority to drive out all demons and to cure diseases, and he sent them out to proclaim the kingdom of God and to heal those who were ill… After this the Lord appointed seventy-two others and sent them two by two ahead of him to every town and place where he was about to go' (Luke 9:1–2; 10:1, NIV).

Jesus was generous. He shared everything he had, including his vision and his mission, and he invited everyone to join in. First, the twelve got the chance to go on an adventure, then the 72. Then, after the day of Pentecost, an open invitation was given to all who believe in Jesus, regardless of nationality, previous faith group, gender or age: young, old, men, women, as Joel had said it would be on the day of the Lord some centuries before (see Joel 2:28). Some radical plans take a long time to come to fruition!

Until then, only the big boys were able to play; now the field was open to everyone. In each generation, we need to fight to give back to the voiceless their rightful place in the mission of Jesus. When people are excluded because of gender, background, race, education or age, we are given the chance to go back to ancient ways and make the church as inclusive as Jesus meant it to be.

Messy Church is part of this pattern of recalibrating churches. The very old are honoured and welcomed and have a purpose, and it's the same for the very young and everyone in between, regardless of gender or background. In fact, 'everyone who calls on the name of the Lord' (Joel 2:32) has a vital role to play in growing the kingdom through their local church.

Is anyone calling on the name of the Lord near you who hasn't yet found a place of belonging in your church?

LUCY MOORE

Everyone's ideas, please!

When Jesus had entered Capernaum, a centurion came to him, asking for help. 'Lord,' he said, 'my servant lies at home paralysed, suffering terribly.' Jesus said to him, 'Shall I come and heal him?' The centurion replied, 'Lord, I do not deserve to have you come under my roof. But just say the word, and my servant will be healed. For I myself am a man under authority, with soldiers under me…' When Jesus heard this, he was amazed and said to those following him, 'Truly I tell you, I have not found anyone in Israel with such great faith'… Then Jesus said to the centurion, 'Go! Let it be done just as you believed it would.' And his servant was healed at that moment.

This outsider really shouldn't have understood anything about the way God works and, frankly, should have been ignored. Spiritually, this centurion must surely have been a complete ignoramus, mustn't he? How could he know anything about the true God when he belonged to a nation of false gods? Imagine how the Jewish listeners were feeling.

But his reply to Jesus' question left Jesus amazed at the centurion's insight. Jesus suddenly saw him not just as a human being in need of compassion, but also as a sign of the opening of the kingdom to people outside the Jewish faith. He even changed his plans to honour the centurion's response.

Being an all-age, inclusive faith community requires us to be receptive when unexpected people express their insights into the things of God. It might mean changing what we were going to do, when, perhaps, children or people with a different belief framework or set of values from our own make suggestions. It requires humility and discernment to sense whether God may be challenging us through their words. But if Jesus could do it, we can.

Make a point today of listening to someone you would normally avoid or ignore.

LUCY MOORE

Allsorts

As [Jesus] walked along, he saw Levi son of Alphaeus sitting at the tax collector's booth. 'Follow me,' Jesus told him, and Levi got up and followed him. While Jesus was having dinner at Levi's house, many tax collectors and sinners were eating with him and his disciples, for there were many who followed him. When the teachers of the law who were Pharisees saw him eating with the sinners and tax collectors, they asked his disciples: 'Why does he eat with tax collectors and sinners?' On hearing this, Jesus said to them, 'It is not the healthy who need a doctor, but those who are ill. I have not come to call the righteous, but sinners.'

What were Jesus' disciples thinking as they reclined around Levi's table? These fellow guests were the sort of people a nice Jewish fisherman's parents would have warned him to stay away from and who would almost certainly incur foot-tapping from that fisherman's wife.

The disciples hadn't been with Jesus very long, after all. Did they trust him not to lead them into dissolute ways among these people, who weren't quite their sort? I mean, a tax collector – a tax collector! And that man leaning across for the mustard, whom you would usually cross the street to avoid. What sort of kingdom was this? What sort of leader was Jesus if he couldn't see who these people were?

Any time we find ourselves wishing somebody wasn't there at church, Messy or otherwise, we need to remember this story and ask ourselves what we're here for and who we're here for. Jesus came for everyone, not just nice, sorted people (as if any of us are). He actively sought and enjoyed the company of people who weren't perfect. He laid himself, his reputation and his disciples down to make a way for everyone to find their way back to God.

Acknowledge any false sense of superiority in yourself towards someone else, and ask Jesus for his forgiveness.

LUCY MOORE

The usefulness of others

Then people brought little children to Jesus for him to place his hands on them and pray for them. But the disciples rebuked them. Jesus said, 'Let the little children come to me, and do not hinder them, for the kingdom of heaven belongs to such as these.' When he had placed his hands on them, he went on from there.

Somebody exclaimed smilingly to me, 'You like children, don't you?' I was a little uncomfortable. 'I like some children,' I said. 'Some, I can't stand. A bit like how I feel about adults, really.' Perhaps I was being unfair. Adults have had more time to make decisions about who they want to be and aspire to be and have had the chance to work on their character. Children are still finding out who they are and who they want to become.

In this encounter, Jesus went way beyond liking or disliking these particular children. He affirmed the right of people of all ages to come close to him. He gave the powerful adults a sharp reminder of the way the kingdom of God should operate, with access to God for everyone, not just the few chosen men. And he affirmed and articulated the children's citizenship of the kingdom, along with the poor in spirit and the persecuted.

When we are an intergenerational church, we have a constant reminder that it's not 'all about me'. We are constantly challenged to make allowances for 'the weaker brethren' of whatever age and to serve, rather than expect to be served. We are constantly challenged to face the fact that God wants people other than ourselves to be close to him and to receive his blessing.

How can you be a blessing today to someone of a different age from your own?

LUCY MOORE

Storykeepers

There was also a prophet, Anna, the daughter of Penuel, of the tribe of Asher. She was very old; she had lived with her husband seven years after her marriage, and then was a widow until she was eighty-four. She never left the temple but worshipped night and day, fasting and praying. Coming up to them at that very moment, she gave thanks to God and spoke about the child to all who were looking forward to the redemption of Jerusalem.

An intergenerational church is one that treasures its older people as well as its younger ones. There's an argument within generational theory that one generation can be of particular help to another specific generation. For instance, the world views of baby boomers (born 1943–60) and millennials (born 1982–2004) resonate in many ways, so millennials are more likely to appreciate mentoring from the boomer generation than from Generation X (born 1961–81). In other words, my young adult children are likely to find the mentoring of someone from my mother's or grandmother's generation more helpful than that of someone from my generation. We need each other.

An intergenerational church expects to be together, to value each other, to need each other and to help each other to enjoy life in all its fullness. The baby Jesus gave to the older woman, Anna, the vindication of a life lived for God and hope for the future of her people. Anna gave Mary and Joseph the reassurance of Jesus' identity under God from her perspective of advanced age and accumulated spiritual wisdom, and she did her bit to pave the way for Jesus' adult ministry, although she would not be there to enjoy it.

*What friendships can you promote safely across the generations
in your church?*

LUCY MOORE

Get out of the way!

[Jesus] said to them, 'Why are you thinking these things? Which is easier: to say to this paralysed man, "Your sins are forgiven," or to say, "Get up, take your mat and walk"? But I want you to know that the Son of Man has authority on earth to forgive sins.' So he said to the man, 'I tell you, get up, take your mat and go home.' He got up, took his mat and walked out in full view of them all. This amazed everyone and they praised God, saying, 'We have never seen anything like this!'

People got in the way of the man on the mat so that he couldn't get to Jesus. Nobody said, 'He needs Jesus more than I do – I'll give up my place in the room so that he can get through.' Nobody offered to pass the mat over the heads of the crowd. It was left to the dogged determination of his friends and their roof-dismantling abilities to get their friend to where he needed to be. Once he was in contact with Jesus, he received healing inside and out and became a new source of amazement and reason for praising God. Until then, he'd been considered merely a nuisance.

We sometimes need to make sacrifices to enable other people to come closer to Jesus. The people in this crowd had every spiritual justification for wanting to be as close to Jesus as possible, but they prevented someone more needy from reaching him. For us, we might be holding on to something equally justifiable and spiritual: a style of singing or praying; a need for silence or for volume; the timing of a service; a style of service that requires a particular leader to be present, taking them away from others. It's worth examining whether any of these might be preventing someone else approaching Jesus and, if so, whether we are prepared to give it up gracefully, believing that seeing God at work in the life of another may make it all worth it.

Ask your church leader if they think there is any way in which you could be helping someone else come closer to Jesus.

LUCY MOORE

Party faith

'Or suppose a woman has ten silver coins and loses one. Doesn't she light a lamp, sweep the house and search carefully until she finds it? And when she finds it, she calls her friends and neighbours together and says, "Rejoice with me; I have found my lost coin." In the same way, I tell you, there is rejoicing in the presence of the angels of God over one sinner who repents.'

Apparently, I have a distinctive laugh. It pops out in public occasionally, to my embarrassment, especially when it happens somewhere like in a cathedral. Outbursts of joy aren't terribly English and are met with disapproval, especially in church – which might be why children have found it so difficult to belong to churches, when they haven't learned to control their joy yet and their glee is met with a 'Shh!'

Do you ever feel embarrassed about the fun, laughter or exuberant joy of the church you belong to? I mean, can it really be church if people are enjoying themselves so much? How quickly we want to get everyone on to the 'real' issues of guilt, repentance, cost, pain and suffering, thoughts of which elicit far more 'appropriate' solemn, churchy responses.

But Jesus shone a light here on a heavenly perspective, which is one of joy, glee and uninhibited community partying based on something real and wonderful to celebrate. People are coming home to God! If the ground state of our churches is one of joy, people will naturally want to join in. They will be swept in willy-nilly. The celebration itself will speak more of God's plan than any carefully worded theology. Partying is at the heart of our faith, and we can rejoice in that truth – and laugh!

Count up the instances of laughter next time you gather as a church or home group. How delighted are you with the result?

LUCY MOORE

Including, excluding

Jesus went up on a mountainside and called to him those he wanted, and they came to him. He appointed twelve that they might be with him and that he might send them out to preach and to have authority to drive out demons. These are the twelve he appointed: Simon (to whom he gave the name Peter); James son of Zebedee and his brother John (to them he gave the name Boanerges, which means 'sons of thunder'), Andrew, Philip, Bartholomew, Matthew, Thomas, James son of Alphaeus, Thaddaeus, Simon the Zealot and Judas Iscariot, who betrayed him.

When Mark wrote his gospel, this exclusively male list of apostles may well have raised no eyebrows, but it does today. We know from other mentions in the gospels that Jesus had female disciples too, so why are none of them appointed here? It can only be conjecture, but we could say that Jesus knew he had to work within the constraints of his culture while paving the way for a more inclusive future. He had such a huge plan, so massive in the scope of change it involved, that it couldn't happen overnight. He deliberately limited himself to what that society could handle, one step at a time.

Sadly, though, all too often through the centuries the church has downplayed, distorted and almost lost the significance of women as equally loved and valued disciples of Christ. How will history judge us as a church? Will we be the ones to play it safe and go with what 'the church' has always done, or will we be faithful to Jesus' world-shaking vision of a kingdom of equality, where the old dividing lines are rubbed out?

Who gets downplayed in our chapter of God's story?

LUCY MOORE

Ezra and Nehemiah

 If a quiz question required a list of the ten best-known books from the Old Testament, it's unlikely that Ezra and Nehemiah would find a place. Yet these small memoirs are highly significant in shining light on the emergence of what we now call the Second Temple Period. These two totally different men, neither born in Jerusalem, one a wealthy and well-connected layman, the other a devout priest and scribe, are nevertheless inextricably linked in the consolidation of Jerusalem as the nucleus for worship and national identity.

Their common purpose was to restore the laws Moses had received from Israel's covenant God, Yahweh, as recorded in Deuteronomy, and secure the nation's freedom from oppression and foreign influences. For the purpose of these notes, it's unnecessary to spend time arguing for a specific date order of events. Our primary focus is to see how Israel's history written by Ezra and Nehemiah speaks across the centuries. We glimpse the startling relevance of their mission and recognise their trials and tribulations as they seek to combat negative strands of human nature which are still causing problems today. Their sky-high ideals triumphed over opposition, jealousy, resentment and betrayal, and their faithfulness to God remains an inspiring testimony of perseverance for every generation.

The exile was seen as the consequence of the people turning away from God. Around 586BC the Babylonian army ransacked Jerusalem, looted and destroyed the temple and took hundreds of people into captivity. Babylon in turn fell to the rising Persian empire. Decades later, thousands of exiles returned to Jerusalem, with Zerubbabel taking the fabulous temple treasures looted by the Babylonians. Several years after the completion of the new, second temple, reports filtered back to Susa – all was not well.

These two books go some way in helping us understand the legalistic attitudes that Jesus found in the scribes, Pharisees, Sadducees and teachers of the law of his day. By that time, the initial laws given to Moses had mushroomed into 613 rigid regulations. Their religion had morphed from awe and obedience into a legalistic straitjacket.

Sit back as we follow Ezra and Nehemiah in their struggles and chart their lasting influence over worship in the holy city and the nation.

ELIZABETH RUNDLE

Setting the scene

'Thus says King Cyrus of Persia: The Lord, the God of heaven, has given me all the kingdoms of the earth, and he has charged me to build him a house at Jerusalem in Judah. Any of those among you who are of his people – may their God be with them! – are now permitted to go up to Jerusalem in Judah, and rebuild the house of the Lord, the God of Israel – he is the God who is in Jerusalem.'

Popular books and TV dramas are these days often enhanced by prequels. Before we plunge into Ezra, let's take a quick overview of the political, social and religious background. About a half-century previously, Nebuchadnezzar, king of Babylon, ransacked and looted the temple in Jerusalem and took hundreds of the population into captivity. Those left behind were spiritually isolated and materially impoverished. After Nebuchadnezzar's death, his empire was soon overcome by the new rising power of Persia.

In the opening verses of Ezra, the writer sees all aspects of life under the prompting of Israel's God, who is Lord of heaven and earth. The edict from Cyrus thus becomes accepted as God's direct prompting rather than a shrewd political move to foster the exiles' loyal compliance and create a kind of buffer zone between Persia and Egypt.

Zerubbabel emerged as the man to lead the returning exiles in the arduous and dangerous journey back to Jerusalem. It's understandable most exiles preferred to remain where they had put down roots and prospered, but they did give generously to the returning group. Gold and silver artefacts in the Israel Museum give us a glimpse of the beauty and artistry of fifth-century BC craftsmen.

Under the personal direction of Zerubbabel, a descendent of King David, the rebuilding of the temple in Jerusalem was begun. First was the altar (Ezra 3:3), which enabled the return of sacrifices, freewill offerings and the rhythm of sacred festivals. The rebuilding would take years of faith and perseverance. It is no secret where Zerubbabel's strength came from.

'Not by might, nor by power, but by my spirit, says the Lord of hosts'
(Zechariah 4:6). Lord, help me to take your words to Zerubbabel as my
guide for today.

ELIZABETH RUNDLE

A solid foundation

When the builders laid the foundation of the temple of the Lord, the priests in their vestments were stationed to praise the Lord with trumpets, and the Levites, the sons of Asaph, with cymbals, according to the directions of King David of Israel; and they sang responsively, praising and giving thanks to the Lord, 'For he is good, for his steadfast love endures for ever towards Israel.'

What a wonderful link with our own time – the returning exiles sang from Psalms (106:1) and still today words from Psalms, either spoken or sung, feature in our worship. This is perhaps because music has the power to touch our emotions way beyond words. In worship, that thin place where humanity seeks to draw close to divinity, words can feel inadequate and restrictive. Music, on the other hand, reaches out over every barrier of age and language, speaking heart to heart and lifting the soul. Ezra 2:65 records among the various returned families that they had 200 singers.

During the lockdowns of 2020–21, when churches were closed, it was the lack of singing people spoke of most. In singing we offer part of ourselves to the corporate worship. I would have loved to witness the musicians praising God by the temple foundations. A truly inspirational event both for those taking part and for those living within sight and earshot of the temple.

So many old buildings – hospitals, libraries, village halls, churches – have a plaque to recall the worthy individual who laid the foundation stone. For the professional builder, the foundation is of paramount importance. These verses convey how little has changed when people seek to mark a momentous occasion – by laying the foundation for the restored temple and thus marking the restoration of the Lord God with his people. What miraculous truth that Christians all over the world still sing in praise and thanksgiving. We still read: 'For no one can lay any foundation other than the one that has been laid; that foundation is Jesus Christ' (1 Corinthians 3:11).

'My heart and voice I raise
to spread Messiah's praise.
Messiah's praise let all repeat.'
(Benjamin Rhodes, 1743–1815)

ELIZABETH RUNDLE

Moving forward

And all the people responded with a great shout when they praised the Lord… But many of the priests and Levites and heads of families, old people who had seen the first house on its foundations, wept with a loud voice when they saw this house, though many shouted aloud for joy, so that the people could not distinguish the sound of the joyful shout from the sound of people's weeping, for the people shouted so loudly that the sound was heard far away.

Oh that little word 'but'. Three letters with such power to deflate. The exiles had returned to the city of their forebears bursting with enthusiasm and hope for the future. By restoring the temple – the house of the Lord God – they engaged in a two-pronged mission. The Lord God would be with them again and they would rededicate themselves to honour and obey his laws. There lay the path to their future prosperity. So you can picture the 'new-comers' vigorously reclaiming the appointed festivals, bringing sacrifices and offerings to God which the inhabitants of the city, members of families not taken captive to Babylon, had abandoned.

I love the telling phrase 'old people who had seen the first house'. The writer evokes a vivid scene with the usual generational problem of disgruntlement that things aren't as good as they were before. Most of us have been on the receiving end of this sort of reception. There is one sure fact we learn as years go by – we can't cling on to the past. The 'now' is the moment we occupy, and ours is the choice to either look back, weep and criticise or move forward, encourage and rejoice. For the Christian, our Lord is not confined to a building but, by mystery and stupendous miracle, is with us at all times and in all places.

Have you ever thought that weeping is a sound understood in every language? The same is true of laughter. Consider other human reactions instantly recognisable across all ages or languages – a touch, a smile, a kindness and the demonstration of that old-fashioned word, compassion.

Lord Jesus, guide me by your Holy Spirit, guard me from despair and fill my heart with your love. Amen

ELIZABETH RUNDLE

Dealing with discouragement

Then the peoples around them set out to discourage the people of Judah and make them afraid to go on building. They bribed the officials to work against them and frustrate their plans during the entire reign of Cyrus king of Persia… Shimshai the secretary wrote a letter against Jerusalem… The king should know that if this city is built and its walls are restored, no more taxes, tribute or duty will be paid, and eventually the royal revenues will suffer.

This chapter of Ezra boils with resentment, jealousy and corruption. The surrounding peoples, those whose families had not been exiled, offered to help build the temple (Ezra 4:2). However, their offer was firmly rebuffed. To find the reason for this we look to 2 Kings 17:41: 'Even while these people were worshipping the Lord, they were serving their idols.' Zerubbabel had no intention of allowing idol worshippers to have any part in rebuilding the holy temple for Israel's one, true God.

Rejection didn't go down well. Tension escalated towards Zerubbabel and the 'newcomers'. Anger stiffened into bullying tactics, which successfully halted the building for years. When a new king, Artaxerxes, came to power in Persia, the aggrieved inhabitants of Samaria (Ezra 4:7–16) concocted a mischievous letter. The king, alarmed at the prospect of Jerusalem regaining power and his revenue slashed, delivered just the order the plotters had hoped for: 'Now issue an order to these men to stop work, so that this city will not be rebuilt until I so order' (Ezra 4:21). Result! Work on rebuilding was stopped – by force (v. 23).

Sadly, insidious bullying creeps into all aspects of life today. Maybe you have experienced tense relationships caused by a letter written in anger, or perhaps a chosen course of action has been blocked by someone's jealousy. It is so easy to be discouraged, to have our physical, mental and spiritual energy evaporate in the face of spite and opposition. But, as we shall see in the next day's notes, when God has a task for us, he equips and enables us. The rebuilding of God's temple was a colossal task, but let's recall the words of our Lord Jesus, 'With God all things are possible' (Matthew 19:26).

Lord, I pray today for all who feel bullied or rejected. Amen

ELIZABETH RUNDLE

'I am with you'

Then Haggai, the messenger of the Lord, spoke to the people with the Lord's message, saying, I am with you, says the Lord. And the Lord stirred up the spirit of Zerubbabel... governor of Judah, and the spirit of Joshua... the high priest, and the spirit of all the remnant of the people; and they came and worked on the house of the Lord of hosts, their God.

The tiny book of the prophet Haggai tells us what happened after the rebuilding work had been stopped: 'Then the word of the Lord came by the prophet Haggai, saying: Is it a time for you yourselves to live in your panelled houses, while this house lies in ruins?' (Haggai 1:3–4). Wood destined to beautify the house of God had obviously been repurposed to panel their own houses.

Sometimes, when we have a prolonged break from a task, we need a jolt to get us motivated to carry on. Into the hearts and minds of the families back from exile, the prophet Haggai was God's instrument for that necessary jolt. What did they think they were doing? Had they forgotten their purpose? It seems as though the enforced halt to rebuilding had deflated the people into apathy. Haggai came on the scene to give just the encouragement they needed to hear – the Lord God said, 'I am with you.'

That wonderful phrase is spoken by the Lord 15 times in the Bible, an affirmation of the Lord's presence at all times and in all places. It's a promise to pour courage into every situation. The temple builders in Jerusalem were able to take up their tools with fresh impetus. This was why they had come 'home' – to restore the temple, the physical manifestation of God's presence with his people. The building would be seen by everyone entering the city as a reminder of the enduring love God had shown to his people. It was a place of sacrifice, prayer and worship, a focal point for the nation.

And that phrase is also Jesus' parting promise to his followers: 'I am with you always' (Matthew 28:20).

Lord Jesus, you know how often my spirit flags. Bless me today with your promise that I may take fresh resolve. Amen

ELIZABETH RUNDLE

Celebrations

Under the preaching of Haggai the prophet and Zechariah… they finished building the temple according to the command of the God of Israel and the decrees of Cyrus, Darius and Artaxerxes, kings of Persia… Then the people of Israel… celebrated the dedication of the house of God with joy… On the fourteenth day of the first month, the exiles celebrated the Passover… For seven days they celebrated with joy.

By mentioning successive Persian kings we get the idea of just how long the temple rebuild had taken – possibly around 15 years. No wonder that when the people saw the completed temple they burst into such rejoicing. Ezra recorded how years of delay, threats, sweat and tears, lethargy and disappointment was finally overcome. Time for national rejoicing.

'On the fourteenth day of the first month, the exiles celebrated the Passover.' Undoubtedly, this major festival, which commemorated the exodus from slavery in Egypt would have taken on extra meaning for the returned exiles. Passover, the Feast of Unleavened Bread, one of the oldest continuously observed religious festivals in the world, celebrated God's hand in Israel's history.

The prophets Haggai and Zechariah made sure that all the inhabitants of Jerusalem remembered God's provision and protection. They encouraged Zerubbabel and his co-leaders, reminding them of God's promises of peace and prosperity: 'I will save you, and you will be a blessing' (Zechariah 8:13).

In times of stress and despondency, we too need a nudge to remember God's promises and blessings. I have been so grateful for gentle reminders to 'keep calm and carry on'. We are not alone; we are co-workers in the mission of building up and encouraging each other. Men, women and children praised the Lord God of Israel on the site where, a few centuries later, Jesus himself would teach and pray. Such is the power of 'place'. Is there a place, church or cathedral where you have felt a certain 'otherness', a 'thin place' which makes you feel calm? Go to that place in your mind now and be encouraged by the prayers of the faithful.

Heavenly Father, thank you for the beauty of holiness
in the places I love. Amen

ELIZABETH RUNDLE

God's guiding hand

After these things, during the reign of Artaxerxes king of Persia… Ezra came up from Babylon. He was a teacher well versed in the law of Moses, which the Lord, the God of Israel, had given. The king had granted him everything he asked, for the hand of the Lord his God was on him.

We are in chapter 7 before Ezra introduces himself – priest, historian, teacher, scribe and descendant of Aaron. The Persian king thought highly of this exiled Israelite, and God would use Ezra's high profile in Babylon, his dedication to the law and his gift of teaching to inspire a spiritual revival centred on the temple in Jerusalem.

It's easy to underestimate the amount of trade and travel between the Middle Eastern countries in those days. Armies, merchants and wandering herdsmen were the main news carriers. Without our luxury of instant news 24/7, people probably received news that was several months old. Living in Babylon, around 900 miles from Jerusalem, Ezra had heard and no doubt rejoiced over the restored temple. King Artaxerxes decided on the magnanimous gesture of allowing Ezra to take any fellow Israelites who wanted to go back to Jerusalem. Not only that but this pagan king also decreed that they take free-will offerings and quantities of gold and silver in order to buy animals for sacrifice once they arrived in Jerusalem. Quite astonishing treasures, plus oil and salt, were catalogued in the king's letter of authority to Ezra (7:11–26).

However, this generous letter ended with the harsh ring of regal power: 'Whoever does not obey the law of your God and the law of the king must surely be punished by death, banishment, confiscation of property, or imprisonment' (v. 26) – a sharp reminder of the sweet carrot and brutal stick employed by powerful empires.

Ezra praised God, convinced that God had touched the king's heart. 'Because the hand of the Lord my God was on me, I took courage' (v. 28). He trusted God's guiding hand as the caravan of Israelites set out on their long journey to Jerusalem.

Guide me, O my great redeemer. Hold me with your mighty hand. Amen

ELIZABETH RUNDLE

Dissension

The leaders came to me and said, 'The people of Israel, including the priests and the Levites, have not kept themselves separate from the neighbouring peoples and their detestable practices… They have taken some of their daughters as wives for themselves and their sons…' When I heard this, I tore my tunic and cloak, pulled hair from my head and beard and sat down appalled.

Of necessity in these short notes, we have skipped over Ezra's journey from Babylon (Ezra 7—8). Suffice to say, his journey began with prayer and faith in God's guidance and protection. And so the exhausted group ('we rested three days', 8:32) arrived in Jerusalem with every treasure intact. Burnt offerings were sacrificed in thanksgiving and King Artaxerxes' letter was delivered to the city officials. So far, so good.

But when things settled down, people went to Ezra to spill the beans on certain activities that were in direct conflict with the law of Moses. To modern minds, Ezra's reaction is over the top. However, we are looking at attitudes of a vastly different time and culture. What was so desperate about taking wives from 'neighbouring peoples'? To religious Israelites, the family was regarded as a complete unit. If either partner wanted to indulge in idol worship, they were both, in the eyes of the law, 'contaminated'.

Cleansing, separation and purity were hallmarks of Abraham's descendants, the basic understanding of Moses and the teaching of priests and Levites. To fall away and follow after other gods was deemed a huge sin, so this was not an ethnic separation but a religious one. Worship of Israel's God was paramount. Ezra knew the book of Deuteronomy better than anyone: 'Do not follow other gods, the gods of the peoples around you; for… his anger will burn against you' (Deuteronomy 6:14–15).

That was the crux of the matter. The temple was rebuilt, worship restored and the people beginning to flourish. It was madness to jeopardise all they had achieved and risk God's anger and further exile. Ezra's mission was to focus the peoples' hearts to worship Israel's God.

Lord, create in me a clean heart and renew a right spirit within me
(from Psalm 51:10). Amen

ELIZABETH RUNDLE

Help from the Lord

While I was in Susa… I asked them about… those who had escaped the captivity, and about Jerusalem. They replied, 'The survivors there in the province who escaped captivity are in great trouble and shame; the wall of Jerusalem is broken down, and its gates have been destroyed by fire.' When I heard these words I sat down and wept, and mourned for days.

We move on several years to meet the other diarist-cum-historian, the Persian king's cup-bearer, Nehemiah. It is likely that Ezra had returned to Babylon for a period as, initially, he is not mentioned. Those who rebuilt the temple had run out of steam when it came to rebuilding the city walls, which left Jerusalem vulnerable. Reading between the lines, if the gates had been burned down, Jerusalem had already suffered hostile attacks.

Far away in Susa, life for Nehemiah at the royal court was comfortable and privileged. Yet deep down, he looked to Jerusalem not only as the home of his ancestors but also as the dwelling place of his God. Nehemiah was distraught to hear the news about the dilapidated state of Jerusalem. Jerusalem – the city of King David – contained the temple built by King Solomon, which was the house of Israel's God. To think of the restored temple exposed and defenceless was unbearable for Nehemiah.

When I was chaplain to the London-Cornish Association, there was a lovely Cornishman who hadn't actually lived in Cornwall for 47 years. Yet Brian's heart beat for Cornwall. In the same way, even though Susa was some thousand miles from Palestine, Nehemiah's heart beat for Jerusalem.

King Artaxerxes immediately noticed his cup-bearer's depression and showed concern. Nehemiah boldly asked permission to go to Jerusalem – to rebuild it (Nehemiah 2:5). Incredibly, king and queen (v. 6) granted permission and gave Nehemiah letters for safe travelling. They also gave him a cavalry escort (vv. 7–9). However, great enthusiasm was not enough. Nehemiah needed help. So he prayed (1:6; 2:4). He sought help from God before anything else. Sometimes our minds are so bursting with what we have or want to do, we forget to pray.

Lord, help me to see how much can be accomplished by prayer and shared responsibility. Amen

ELIZABETH RUNDLE

Take your time…

When Sanballat the Horonite and Tobiah the Ammonite official heard about this, they were very much disturbed that someone had come to promote the welfare of the Israelites. I went to Jerusalem, and after staying there three days I set out during the night with a few others. I had not told anyone what my God had put in my heart to do for Jerusalem.

Yesterday, we could imagine the prayerful Nehemiah and his cavalry escort riding off towards the horizon to the sound of an atmospheric film score. Today, the music changes. From caves in a ridge, two shadowy figures watch and wait as the rhythm throbs with menace.

At that time Samaria and Judah were separate provinces, and in ancient Hebrew documents found in Egypt, Sanballat is named as governor of neighbouring Samaria. To recap on Ezra 4:3, Zerubbabel had rejected Samaritan help in rebuilding the temple. That rejection caused a toxic rift, which festered over time. Tobiah may have held some official responsibility for Jerusalem. The sight of the Persian king's cup-bearer, with an army escort, enflamed their hostility. At best, it signalled gross interference; at worst, a precursor to further invasion. Their own personal power and authority was threatened.

James Bond films have an avid, worldwide audience, which proves the enduring popularity of spy stories. Spies have always been around, and the court of Artaxerxes would have received reports from agents all across the ever-widening empire. Nehemiah's actions on arrival in Jerusalem indicate that he was not naive to this situation. He took three days to lower the profile of his arrival and kept secret his reason for being in the city. He decided to take a quiet look for himself at the state of the walls. Under cover of night, he made a calm evaluation of the broken walls and burned-down city gates.

This level-headed approach is a good example to follow. It's good to resist the temptation to rush at a situation, for so much more is achieved by a calm, prayerful approach.

Lord, help me learn from these ancient stories, these mirrors of human nature. Guide me today as you guided your people then. Amen

ELIZABETH RUNDLE

Faithful in prayer

I gave them my report: 'Face it: we're in a bad way here. Jerusalem is a wreck... Come – let's build the wall of Jerusalem and not live with this disgrace any longer.' I told them how God was supporting me... They said, 'We're with you. Let's get started'... When Sanballat the Horonite, Tobiah the Ammonite official, and Geshem the Arab heard about it, they laughed at us...

Nehemiah possessed a persuasive, charismatic personality. In his address to the assembled priests and inhabitants, he made it plain that the gracious hand of God was on him (v. 18). Such was the power of Nehemiah's vision, he managed to motivate the people, priests and officials to agree to get stuck in to repair the city walls. His combined humility and piety enthused the dispirited people in the city and surrounding villages, and they rallied to his call. The NRSV states: 'They committed themselves to the common good' (v. 18).

In biblical terms 'the common good' means inclusive caring for the most vulnerable, the forgotten and the least, as well as the strong. Nehemiah and Ezra based their faith on the moral teaching in Deuteronomy, a teaching fulfilled by our Lord Jesus when he taught people to love their neighbours as themselves (Mark 12:30–31) and to treat others as they would want to be treated (Matthew 7:12). 'The common good' stands like a timeless, global recipe for the improved well-being of all. (Compare the United Nations Millennium Project.) Nehemiah saw the need for solid defences around the city. Only then would it be a secure dwelling place for Israel's God.

However, all was not sweetness and light. Sanballat and Tobiah had found a new ally – Geshem. Mocking and sniggering, they constantly tried to undermine Nehemiah's authority and the morale of his builders. Tobiah had a great line: 'Even a fox climbing up on it would break down their wall of stones!' (4:3, NIV). Among the builders were priests, perfumers, goldsmiths and even some daughters. Throughout the building, Sanballat, Tobiah and Geshem kept up a barrage of intimidation, false accusations, rumours and plots. Against all this Nehemiah prayed to God and stayed resolute.

Lord, when things don't go as planned, give me strength to pray. Amen

ELIZABETH RUNDLE

Problems pile up

There were those who said, 'We are having to borrow money on our fields and vineyards to pay the king's tax… our children are the same as their children; and yet we are forcing our sons and daughter to be slaves, and some of our daughters have been ravished; we are powerless, and our fields and vineyards now belong to others.' I was very angry when I heard their outcry and these complaints.

During the 52 days it took to rebuild the city walls, crises lunged at Nehemiah from all sides. Time spent building up the broken walls meant the people had neglected their own houses, fields, vineyards and olive groves. Nehemiah records 'a great outcry of the people and of their wives against their Jewish kin' (5:1). They were desperate.

To understand Nehemiah's fury, we have to recognise God's word had been blatantly ignored by Israelites who had put profit before moral duty: 'If any of your fellow Israelites become poor and are unable to support themselves among you, help them… Do not take interest or any profit from them, but fear your God… Do not make them work as slaves' (Leviticus 25:35–39, NIV); 'I command you to be open-handed towards your fellow Israelites who are poor and needy in your land' (Deuteronomy 15:11, NIV). Behind Nehemiah's back, God's commands had been disobeyed.

God's concern for the poor runs through nearly every one of the Bible's 66 books, yet the poor and marginalised remain a constant sorrow. What a sad indictment on our 'modern' world that corruption, exploitation, child-trafficking and slavery retain their claws deep in every continent.

Nehemiah called 'a great assembly' (5:7) and sternly read the riot act. From this chapter, we learn two things about him: his unstinting generosity and the fact he never took allowances due to him as governor.

With one problem sorted, Nehemiah then faced another. Sanballat and Geshem accused him of wanting to be king; that is, treason. Tobiah sent intimidating letters and several false prophets sought to undermine Nehemiah's mission. Nehemiah poured out his heart to God in prayer.

Dear Lord, I pray for courage to face any hurtful words
or false accusations. Amen

ELIZABETH RUNDLE

Wall-to-wall rejoicing

I also assigned two large choirs to give thanks. One was to proceed on top of the wall to the right... with musical instruments prescribed by David the man of God. Ezra the teacher of the Law led the procession... The second choir proceeded in the opposite direction. I followed them on top of the wall... The two choirs that gave thanks then took their places in the house of God; so did I.

At last! The wall surrounding Jerusalem was rebuilt and strong enough for processions to march along the top. Nehemiah organised a praise spectacular the people would never forget. Ezra the priest and scribe, by then an elderly man, was given the honour to lead one choir, while Nehemiah followed the second choir (v. 38). Verse 43 records that 'the sound of rejoicing in Jerusalem could be heard far away'. Nehemiah made sure Sanballat, Tobiah and Geshem would know that the people who worshipped the God of Abraham had triumphed in the face of all their opposition.

Much of Nehemiah's memoir is taken up by lengthy, detailed lists – genealogical records of the first exiles to return – priests, Levites, gatekeepers, musicians and temple servants – as well as a catalogue of donkeys, camels, horses and mules. He also recorded donations of priestly garments, gold and silver. In chapter 8, we meet Ezra reading the book of the law of Moses to an attentive crowd 'from daybreak till noon' (8:3). The people were truly moved by God's word and entered into a solemn covenant to obey 'all the commands, regulations and decrees of the Lord our God' (10:29). They promised their daughters would not marry people who didn't worship Israel's God and vowed to keep the Sabbath. Nehemiah was a form-filler par excellence. His meticulous records give us a fascinating overview of how the city was restored. However, we know with hindsight what Nehemiah and Ezra could only suspect – good intentions are all too easily forgotten.

After the public display of joy, choirs and musicians paraded into the temple. Inspired and sustained by the 'hand of God', Ezra and Nehemiah celebrated the culmination of their life's work in praise and thanksgiving.

Thank you, Lord, for bringing me to this day.
May it be filled with praise and thanksgiving. Amen

ELIZABETH RUNDLE

God first

Then Nehemiah the governor, Ezra the priest and teacher of the Law, and the Levites who were instructing the people said to them all, 'This day is holy to the Lord your God'… Then all the people went away to eat and drink, to send portions of food and to celebrate with great joy, because they now understood the words that had been made known to them.

Neither Ezra nor Nehemiah had prophetic visions or messianic dreams. They devoutly followed God's law given to Moses in the book we call Deuteronomy. Their God was perceived in a narrow, nationalistic sense, with moral duty to the law the only means to peace and prosperity. Both men were driven by the sense of God's hand upon them and, by prayer and fasting, dedicated themselves to right Israel's wrongs.

We have to remind ourselves that we are gazing way back into a nation's history. So much appears archaic, even ruthless, yet, rather than taking a judgemental approach, it's worthwhile to note parallels with our own time. Both Ezra and Nehemiah saw the state of Jerusalem as a direct result of the people's neglect of worship and their involvement with other groups who cared nothing for Yahweh, Israel's God. Their sincerity, courage and absolute devotion to restoring Jerusalem to its former status is beyond reproach, but we cannot overlook the ruthlessness shown to foreigners and the bitterness that seeps into some prayers (Ezra 10:3; Nehemiah 2:20).

Today's politicians are much concerned with their legacy. Our two characters were more concerned with what they could change there and then. The whole point of their considerable personal sacrifice was to educate their people to honour God and his temple, to rediscover the discipline of the various sacrifices and festivals and maintain the purity of their nation. In other words, they sought to change hearts and minds from love of self to love of God. Thank God there are people this very moment with that same vision, enriched by the knowledge and love of the Saviour of the world, Jesus Christ, our Lord. What kind of legacy will you leave?

Jesus said, 'Love the Lord your God with all your heart and…
love your neighbour as yourself' (Matthew 22:37, 39).

ELIZABETH RUNDLE

James

Let endurance have its full effect, so that you may be mature and complete, lacking in nothing.

JAMES 1:4 (NRSV)

 One of the things about the Bible that should no longer surprise me is the regularity with which I read verses, passages or even whole books that seem like they were written yesterday, that speak directly to current issues or offer a challenge or, less often, a solution to a contemporary concern.

For me, the book of James is one such example. It's a letter that doesn't pull its punches, that goes to the heart of so many of the societal challenges that we're facing right now and calls on us to meet them in a countercultural way. It's a letter that advocates perseverance and endurance rather than short cuts, that calls us to examine the way we use our power to the benefit or detriment of others and that reminds our social media-obsessed world to watch the way we use our words.

But it's also a letter that can challenge some of our most fundamental beliefs about what it means to live as a Christian. James isn't interested in right belief in isolation; James is interested in seeing right belief flowing over into right action. And while his first readers might have lived lives that were, on the surface, very different from our own, they faced many of the same practical, social and ethical issues that we face almost 2,000 years later.

Over these next two weeks, we'll consider how James might challenge us to rethink how we speak, how we shop, our preconceptions about the people we meet and, by extension, how we treat them.

While this letter speaks to us as individuals, there are also significant implications for the wider Christian community. As we think about what our own response might be, we also need to engage with how God might be calling us to help shape the Christian community of which we are a part. As the church continues to reimagine its calling in the light of the Covid-19 pandemic, what might the book of James offer us, both as the community of God's people – his hands and feet in the world – and as individual Christians?

LOUISE DAVIS

Life is tough

My brothers and sisters, whenever you face trials of any kind, consider it nothing but joy, because you know that the testing of your faith produces endurance; and let endurance have its full effect, so that you may be mature and complete, lacking in nothing. If any of you is lacking in wisdom, ask God, who gives to all generously and ungrudgingly, and it will be given you.

When my nieces and nephew were small, one of their go-to bedtime stories was Michael Rosen's brilliantly simple tale of a family who go on a bear hunt. On every page they are confronted by challenges that lie between them and the next stage of their journey. They consider going over, under and around the problem, but each time they realise the challenge can only be overcome by going through it.

There are a few themes that will crop up repeatedly as we work our way through the book of James over the next two weeks, and these four verses introduce one of them: enduring through trials. We can't go over, under or around the trials we face; we have to go through them, and in doing so we develop endurance.

Trials are a fact of life, be they large or small, personal or global, of our own making or out of our control. These verses remind us that we have a choice about how we might navigate our way through them: resenting the experience from beginning to end or making a conscious decision to celebrate the opportunity for personal growth and the deepening of our faith – becoming 'mature and complete' – that so often comes as a result of the most difficult times of our lives.

But these verses also remind us that we're not left to our own devices. On the contrary, God gives wisdom 'generously and ungrudgingly' to all who ask. In choosing to acknowledge our agency and ask for God's help, we begin to see how we might just consider those times 'nothing but joy'.

Generous God, we know from experience that trials are a fact of life. We thank you for your promise of the wisdom to navigate our way through them, and of maturity as we learn from them. Amen

LOUISE DAVIS

Look pain in the face

Blessed is anyone who endures temptation. Such a one has stood the test and will receive the crown of life that the Lord has promised to those who love him. No one, when tempted, should say, 'I am being tempted by God'; for God cannot be tempted by evil and he himself tempts no one. But one is tempted by one's own desire, being lured and enticed by it; then, when that desire has conceived, it gives birth to sin, and that sin, when it is fully grown, gives birth to death. Do not be deceived, my beloved.

'I can resist anything except temptation.' So announces Lord Darlington in Oscar Wilde's 1892 play *Lady Windermere's Fan*. It's a sentiment I often find myself agreeing with! Today's reading picks up the theme of endurance that we explored yesterday, but the author's attention has turned from trials to temptation.

It's interesting that James doesn't offer any examples of 'temptations' here. I wonder whether that's because he's talking less about a temptation to indulge in a specific sin and more about human nature's predisposition to taking the easy option in any given circumstance.

I recently listened to a fascinating conversation with country music icon Dolly Parton. Contrary to the popular perception of Parton as a 'lightweight' artist, interviewer Brené Brown reflected on the fact that many of her guest's songs deal with big issues, including suicide and abuse. Dolly, she said, is a songwriter who's willing to look pain in the face and not turn away.

In light of what we have already discovered about the value of enduring through trials, perhaps this observation sheds helpful light on how we might understand this passage. We live our lives surrounded by messages that tell us that we can avoid hard things, difficult people and experiences that cause us pain, and it's tempting to believe that the solutions offered by the world will enable us to steer a path around things that challenge us.

Perhaps we instead need to follow Dolly's example, choosing to look pain in the face and not turn away.

God of compassion, when we are tempted to find easy solutions to the challenges of life, give us the strength to resist and to endure. Amen

LOUISE DAVIS

Listen, listen, listen

You must understand this, my beloved: let everyone be quick to listen, slow to speak, slow to anger; for your anger does not produce God's righteousness. Therefore rid yourselves of all sordidness and rank growth of wickedness, and welcome with meekness the implanted word that has the power to save your souls.

One of the major news stories of 2021 was footballer Marcus Rashford's campaign to change the UK government's response to child food poverty. I recently watched a BBC documentary about the campaign, and one of the things that struck me the most was Rashford's commitment to listening, in particular to the stories of those whose experience of food poverty – including his own – would enable him to make a case for change.

He listens to teachers, parents and children impacted by food poverty, to those running the breakfast clubs and food banks on which they rely, to charities and other organisations campaigning on the same issues and even to the UK's major supermarket chains. One of the most quietly profound moments comes when, en route home from playing for his club, Manchester United, he receives a phone call from the prime minister, Boris Johnson. We hear little of both sides of the conversation, and I'm struck by the fact that, even now, Rashford is listening rather than speaking.

I was also struck by the fact that throughout the documentary, which I realise has been heavily edited to tell a particular story, we never see Marcus Rashford angry, despite his evident depth of feeling about the issues at hand and his unwavering commitment to do something about them.

We're all familiar with the idea that because people have two ears and one mouth they should listen twice as much as they talk, and I think that's a sentiment James would have a lot of time for. But James goes a step further here in his warning against being too quick to give way to anger. It's a reminder that it's not enough just to listen; we have to respond appropriately to what we hear.

Loving God, today may I be quick to listen – to you and to those around me – slow to speak and slow to anger. Amen

LOUISE DAVIS

Right listening, right responses, right action

But be doers of the word, and not merely hearers who deceive themselves. For if any are hearers of the word and not doers, they are like those who look at themselves in a mirror; for they look at themselves and, on going away, immediately forget what they were like. But those who look into the perfect law, the law of liberty, and persevere, being not hearers who forget but doers who act – they will be blessed in their doing.

Back in the early 1990s, the Christian band du jour, DC Talk, released an album which included a track entitled 'Luv Is a Verb', a call to arms for a generation of young people who wanted their faith to make a difference to the way they lived their lives day-by-day. Thirty years later, it's a sentiment I come back to regularly, and I think it sits at the heart of this passage.

I grew up in a church that elevated the reading, studying and exposition of scripture above almost everything else. It's left me with a Bible that has key 'proof texts' underlined in biro, and a sense of deep discombobulation at sermons that are shorter than 20 minutes! So I'm grateful for the challenge of bands like DC Talk that taught me really early on that all that 'head knowledge' was of limited value if it wasn't translated into action.

In these verses, James moves from warning his audience to guard against the negative impact of what we hear to encouraging positive action. I suspect that many of us struggle with our perception of the extent of our own agency. In the face of apparently intractable global, local and even personal challenges, it can be incredibly easy to feel overwhelmed and useless. I love the apocryphal story of the person who, while walking along a beach covered in stranded starfish struggling for life, comes across a child who is determinedly picking up starfish one by one and throwing them back into the sea. 'Why are you doing that? You can't save all the starfish,' they ask the child. 'No,' the child replies, 'but I can save that one. And that one. And that one.'

Who or what are the starfish to whom you can make a difference today?
What one small action can you take?

LOUISE DAVIS

Back to basics

If any think they are religious, and do not bridle their tongues but deceive their hearts, their religion is worthless. Religion that is pure and undefiled before God, the Father, is this: to care for orphans and widows in their distress, and to keep oneself unstained by the world.

Today's passage follows neatly on from yesterday's rallying cry to be doers of the word and not just hearers. It sounds so simple, doesn't it? To care for widows and orphans and keep oneself from being defiled by the world. Yet it's one of those passages that when you start pulling at the thread it just keeps unravelling.

Archbishop Desmond Tutu famously said of social action, 'There comes a point where we need to stop just pulling people out of the river. We need to go upstream and find out why they're falling in.' Care for 'widows and orphans' – the most vulnerable in society – isn't just about doing individual good works; it's about systemic change.

Living as we do in an age of 24-hour news, television and film streaming services and social media, we are subject to a constant barrage of messages telling us what we should buy, who we should listen to and how we should spend our time. Many of us would agree that the dominant messages coming at us from these sources – and even from our politicians, broadsheet newspapers and the mainstream media – are not conducive to keeping oneself 'unstained by the world'. And while I'm sure we'd all like to think that we are immune to this messaging, we're not!

I wonder whether these verses are a call not just to engage in our own small, individual 'acts of kindness' in caring for the most vulnerable in society, but also to actively work to subvert the ethics, values and assumptions of the world in which we live.

God of justice, open my eyes to see the 'orphans and widows' who cross my path today and show me how I might care for them. But show me, too, how I might challenge the structures and systems that allow the most vulnerable in society to become trapped in poverty and deprivation. Amen

LOUISE DAVIS

Favouritism

My brothers and sisters, do you with your acts of favouritism really believe in our glorious Lord Jesus Christ? For if a person with gold rings and in fine clothes comes into your assembly, and if a poor person in dirty clothes also comes in, and if you take notice of the one wearing the fine clothes and say, 'Have a seat here, please', while to the one who is poor you say, 'Stand there', or, 'Sit at my feet', have you not made distinctions among yourselves, and become judges with evil thoughts?

It was Homeless Sunday at a local church committed to social justice in many forms. Many of the homeless people involved in its projects were invited to attend, and several did. Coincidentally, the church's Friends organisation was being celebrated at the same service, and so this very different group was also invited. As people took their seats, I realised the Friends had chairs reserved for them at the front, while the homeless guests were dotted around the congregation. As the service began, the group of Friends were warmly welcomed but no such welcome was extended to the other special group of guests. And so on.

I'd love to tell you that this story is a parable, but it isn't. In a church genuinely committed to justice and inclusion, on the Sunday when you could argue it mattered the most, it failed to live out that commitment in the most basic way.

The reality, of course, is that we all show favouritism. Those who think and write about issues around race, gender and sexuality explore the idea of 'unconscious bias'; this same unconscious bias impacts the decisions we make about accommodating homeless people and Friends in the same service, or who we'll invite for dinner, or which people we'd prefer as next-door neighbours.

As the American activist James Baldwin pointed out, 'Not everything that is faced can be changed, but nothing can be changed until it is faced.' Until we face the fact that we all do 'acts of favouritism' – consciously or otherwise – we will never change.

God of all, forgive me for the many times when unconscious bias has blinded me to your image in those around me. Help me to change. Amen

LOUISE DAVIS

Dishonour and partiality

Listen, my beloved brothers and sisters. Has not God chosen the poor in the world to be rich in faith and to be heirs of the kingdom that he has promised to those who love him? But you have dishonoured the poor. Is it not the rich who oppress you? Is it not they who drag you into court? Is it not they who blaspheme the excellent name that was invoked over you? You do well if you really fulfil the royal law according to the scripture, 'You shall love your neighbour as yourself.' But if you show partiality, you commit sin and are convicted by the law as transgressors.

Yesterday we explored how easy it is to find ourselves seduced into favouritism, and today's verses pick up this theme and challenge us to consider how we might push back against this.

It seems to me that most of us are predisposed to give greater honour to those who have more: more money, more power, more 'stuff'. We think that if we invest time and energy in cultivating a relationship with them, they'll bathe us in their reflected glory. Ironically, as these verses point out, it's also those with more who have the power to oppress others, and so these verses hold up a mirror to our instincts to align ourselves with the 'haves'. They remind us that, since our highest calling as the people of God is to love our neighbour as ourselves, we should be investing our time, attention and energy into those who can't do anything for us.

And there is an implicit invitation here to be the support and encouragement others need us to be during their own trials and temptations. In fact, the passage reminds us of what we've already learnt this week, that enduring through hard times builds a richness of faith. When we choose to invest our time and energy into relationships of mutual encouragement and support – in 'doing life' with others, sharing the tough times and the blessings – everyone benefits.

God of the 'haves' and the 'have nots', when we're tempted to cultivate relationships for our own benefit, remind us of the countercultural nature of your kingdom. Amen

LOUISE DAVIS

Faith and works

What good is it, my brothers and sisters, if you say you have faith but do not have works? Can faith save you? If a brother or sister is naked and lacks daily food, and one of you says to them, 'Go in peace; keep warm and eat your fill', and yet you do not supply their bodily needs, what is the good of that? So faith by itself, if it has no works, is dead. But someone will say, 'You have faith and I have works.' Show me your faith without works, and I by my works will show you my faith. You believe that God is one; you do well. Even the demons believe – and shudder.

I grew up in a church with an almost contradictory approach to the relationship between 'faith' and 'works'. Conservative – both socially and theologically – and evangelical, the focus of all our services, Sunday School meetings and children's holiday clubs was firmly on 'becoming a Christian', on praying a prayer inviting Jesus into your heart and gaining your ticket to heaven. And yet, I also had it drummed into me that my faith didn't – couldn't – stop at my own personal relationship with Jesus; it had to have a positive impact on the lives of those around me.

I believe that 'works' are an integral part of the calling of every Christian to live out the values of the kingdom of God in the world around us. What that looks like will be different for each of us, shaped by our circumstances, our resources, our relationships, our experiences, our gifts and talents… the list goes on.

However, almost inconceivably, we still live in a world where huge numbers of people go hungry everyday and have nowhere to live. Even here in the UK, food-bank use and homelessness have been on the rise. That the challenge of this passage should still apply to us in its most literal sense in the 21st century seems extraordinary. How might we show our faith by our actions on behalf of the most vulnerable in our nation and our world?

God of the poor, the hungry, the homeless, give me the courage to show my faith by what I do practically for those most in need. Amen

LOUISE DAVIS

Great power, great responsibility

How great a forest is set ablaze by a small fire! And the tongue is a fire. The tongue is placed among our members as a world of iniquity; it stains the whole body, sets on fire the cycle of nature, and is itself set on fire by hell. For every species of beast and bird, of reptile and sea creature, can be tamed and has been tamed by the human species, but no one can tame the tongue – a restless evil, full of deadly poison.

My two youngest sisters have an excellent recall of great quotes from films. There are a number of characteristics I share with my sisters; this is not one of them! My quote repertoire runs to two, one from *Sister Act* and one from 2002's *Spider-Man*: 'With great power comes great responsibility.'

The rapid increase in the scope of the internet means that greater numbers of people than ever have the opportunity to make their voices heard. Traditional media, such as radio, television, newspapers and magazines, are rapidly being eclipsed by a proliferation of social media outlets, video channels and podcasts. One of the great benefits of this new media is that voices that have traditionally struggled to make themselves heard are now able to contribute in new ways. But the louder the noise, the greater the tension between the power to make our own voice heard and the responsibility we have to listen to the voices of others.

That same tension resides in our everyday encounters. Every time we speak to or communicate with another person, we exercise power: the power to make someone feel welcome or worthless, to educate or oppress. The call to tame our tongues has rarely been more urgent or more countercultural.

Today, think about how you might use the power of your voice for the benefit of someone, or something, less powerful than you.

Loving God, help me choose my words carefully today, aware of the responsibility that comes with their power. In the noise of a world which clamours for my attention, open my ears to hear voices I have overlooked or ignored.

LOUISE DAVIS

Be better

Who is wise and understanding among you? Show by your good life that your works are done with gentleness born of wisdom. But if you have bitter envy and selfish ambition in your hearts, do not be boastful and false to the truth. Such wisdom does not come down from above, but is earthly, unspiritual, devilish. For where there is envy and selfish ambition, there will also be disorder and wickedness of every kind. But the wisdom from above is first pure, then peaceable, gentle, willing to yield, full of mercy and good fruits, without a trace of partiality or hypocrisy. And a harvest of righteousness is sown in peace for those who make peace.

One of my favourite television shows of the past few years is *W1A*, the spoof documentary series about life at the BBC. The show beautifully sends up the jargon-ridden, catchphrase-cultivating corporate culture that can develop in any organisation. But there is one job title that makes complete sense to me: director of better. Significant airtime is taken up with discussing what the 'better' in this job title might be, but I'm not sure it really matters.

I think the author's exhortation to his readers in this passage is simply to be better: to cultivate a wisdom that leads them to become people who truly embody and live out the values of the kingdom of God. He's spent time over the previous couple of chapters exploring what that might look like, and these verses read like a closing argument that reminds the reader that all of our listening and activity needs to be imbued with godly wisdom.

This wisdom is 'peaceable, gentle, willing to yield, full of mercy and good fruits, without a trace of partiality or hypocrisy'. James isn't talking about things we choose to do in the moment, in response to a specific incident or circumstance. Rather, he is referring to things that are deeply ingrained in who we are – the values out of which we make tough choices, even when under duress. Being better is a character issue.

Loving God, help us to be people who strive to be better, who cultivate your wisdom and live it out through good works done with gentleness. Amen

LOUISE DAVIS

Deo volente

Come now, you who say, 'Today or tomorrow we will go to such and such a town and spend a year there, doing business and making money.' Yet you do not even know what tomorrow will bring. What is your life? For you are a mist that appears for a little while and then vanishes. Instead you ought to say, 'If the Lord wishes, we will live and do this or that.' As it is, you boast in your arrogance; all such boasting is evil. Anyone, then, who knows the right thing to do and fails to do it, commits sin.

When I was a teenager, our church appointed a new minister. He was a prolific note- and letter-writer and would send tens of missives each week to those in the congregation. I was the recipient of a good number – many received after I became a trainee youth worker at the church – and those which contained suggestions or arrangements for future meetings or activities all concluded the same way: DV – *Deo volente*. God willing.

I suspect that many of us found ourselves praying 'DV' – consciously or otherwise – a great deal during our recent shared experience of living through a global pandemic. For many of us, the uncertainty of life during Covid-19 has been, as we are regularly reminded by politicians, pundits and the media, unprecedented. It has stripped us of the veneer of control over our lives that so many of us take for granted.

Reading these verses today, I'm aware that my response to them feels quite different to the one I would have had pre-Covid-19. Having seen our lives change so much over the course of just a few short weeks at the beginning of 2020, I now have a very different perspective on the idea that I am 'a mist that appears for a little while and then vanishes'.

The challenge, of course, is to strike a balance between acknowledging that we don't know what tomorrow will bring and therefore learning to sit light to the challenges and opportunities that each day presents, while not using that perspective as an excuse for laziness or complacency.

Omniscient God, we trust an unknown future to you, knowing that you walk with us through all that lies ahead. Amen

LOUISE DAVIS

Who are the rich?

Come now, you rich people, weep and wail for the miseries that are coming to you. Your riches have rotted, and your clothes are moth-eaten. Your gold and silver have rusted, and their rust will be evidence against you, and it will eat your flesh like fire. You have laid up treasure for the last days. Listen! The wages of the labourers who mowed your fields, which you kept back by fraud, cry out, and the cries of the harvesters have reached the ears of the Lord of hosts. You have lived on the earth in luxury and in pleasure; you have fattened your hearts on a day of slaughter. You have condemned and murdered the righteous one, who does not resist you.

Who are the 'rich' in these verses? I'm sure I'm not the only person who instinctively wants to identity with the 'goodies' in any biblical narrative. In my defence, I don't have a field that I employ people to work in, so the 'rich people' of this passage can't possibly include me. Can it?

Except that every time I buy something in a supermarket, I also buy into the trade, farming and processing values of the companies who produce each item of food or clothing, each cleaning product. Those of us who are privileged enough to make choices about where and how we shop also have a responsibility to make choices about how we spend our money and the kind of values we want to uphold.

From fair trade and eco credentials to animal welfare and shopping locally, our power as consumers is vast. The reality is that shopping intentionally, of making conscious choices to ensure our consumption does less damage than it might, will cost us, both financially and in the time it takes to find and choose 'good' options.

However, the cost to people and the planet is far higher if we don't take that time and spend that money. If our faith is to make a difference to the way we live, choosing to shop ethically is about both the now and the not yet of the kingdom of God.

Generous God, as I make choices about how to use my resources, make me mindful of the impact these have on those I will never meet. Amen

LOUISE DAVIS

Patience and endurance

Be patient, therefore, beloved, until the coming of the Lord. The farmer waits for the precious crop from the earth, being patient with it until it receives the early and the late rains. You also must be patient. Strengthen your hearts, for the coming of the Lord is near. Beloved, do not grumble against one another, so that you may not be judged. See, the Judge is standing at the doors! As an example of suffering and patience, beloved, take the prophets who spoke in the name of the Lord. Indeed we call blessed those who showed endurance. You have heard of the endurance of Job, and you have seen the purpose of the Lord, how the Lord is compassionate and merciful.

My love of gardening began as a small child when I was introduced to Mary Lennox and her friends Dickon and Colin (*The Secret Garden*, Frances Hodgson Burnett, 1911). Their discovery of a secret garden and their shared experience of its power to bring physical and emotional healing captured my heart and my imagination. My dad read the story to me each evening from the red presentation edition I was given by my grandparents for my seventh birthday.

Over the four years in which I've lived in my current house – a terrace with a very small outside space at the back – I've slowly transformed a yard into a garden, building raised beds and cultivating both ornamental plants and, increasingly, fruit and vegetables. Patience and endurance are as integral to the experience of gardening as they are for the farmer in these verses, although it's fair to say that the inevitable failures I experience in the garden have fewer potentially catastrophic consequences than those experienced, even today, by those involved in agriculture.

Gardening has taught me not only to wait, but also to recognise signs of life, particularly in the long, dark days of winter. Weeks – sometimes months – before any flowers will appear, green shoots begin to emerge from the cold ground; I'm reminded that good things are coming and that the waiting will be worth it.

Compassionate and merciful God, thank you that even when you seem
far off, we can see signs of the coming of your kingdom. Amen

LOUISE DAVIS

The power of prayer

Are any among you suffering? They should pray. Are any cheerful? They should sing songs of praise. Are any among you sick? They should call for the elders of the church and have them pray over them, anointing them with oil in the name of the Lord. The prayer of faith will save the sick, and the Lord will raise them up; and anyone who has committed sins will be forgiven. Therefore confess your sins to one another, and pray for one another, so that you may be healed. The prayer of the righteous is powerful and effective. Elijah was a human being like us, and he prayed fervently that it might not rain, and for three years and six months it did not rain on the earth. Then he prayed again, and the heaven gave rain and the earth yielded its harvest.

I first came across the idea that 'God only has our hands and feet to change the world' in the mid-noughties, when I went to work for a church in an Urban Priority Area in east London. Situated in a deprived area that had been first devastated by bombing during World War II and then blighted by the unemployment which resulted from the closure of the docks, this church knew that making a difference to the lives of those in their community meant getting its hands dirty.

It was – and still is – a church that knew how to live out so much of the rallying cry to action that we've read about in James. But this final reading reminds us that in all our hard graft – and we are called to hard graft – we must never lose sight of the fact that it is God's work we're doing. It serves as a reminder that, while each of us has a practical role to play in bringing God's kingdom to bear in our world and our communities, it is, ultimately, something we are unable to do except through the work of the Holy Spirit.

We thank you, God, that you call us to work with you to bring your kingdom to bear in our world. Give us your eyes and your perspective as we seek to be your hands and your feet to those around us. Amen

LOUISE DAVIS

Babylon

 To adventurous travellers, 'Babylon' means the archaeo-
logical site in Iraq; to cultural commentators, it is a useful
shorthand for decadence and excess; to Christian and Jewish
believers, it means the place of physical exile and also a
symbolic earthly power in defiant opposition to the Almighty.
Turning to the Bible, we find reference to Babylon in some guise or other
from Genesis to Revelation. The dramatic history and profound desolation
surrounding Judah's sixth-century BC Babylonian exile have inspired countless works of art and music. The Hanging Gardens of Babylon were listed
as one of the seven wonders of the ancient world, along with the Great
Pyramid of Giza and the Colossus of Rhodes.

In working on these readings, I've been reminded of the significance of
place for our faith. The story of God's working in the world is, for the most
part, precisely located in the countries in and around the eastern Mediterranean. Learning about the historical and geographical background helps
to broaden our understanding of what we believe and why. I've also realised
the importance of allowing a prophetic word or symbol to resonate beyond
its original context. Yes, Babylon meant that ancient Near Eastern city, but
it was also used to refer to Rome, and there are still Babylon-like places
and powers to be encountered today.

As with reading so much of the Bible, we need to strike a balance
between discerning the author's original intention and what we can learn
for our walk as disciples today. If an idea or passage seems too remote
from our context, we may be tempted to dismiss it altogether, bypassing
it in search of a more accessible passage. We may even come up with a
convoluted interpretation to allow some application to life today (which
may end up doing more harm than good). Wisdom is called for, as indicated
by the helpful bidding often used after Bible readings in Anglican services:
'Hear what the Spirit is saying to the church.' As you reflect on 'Babylon' over
the next two weeks, I pray that you may be open to what the Spirit might
be saying to you and, in doing so, find both inspiration and consolation.

NAOMI STARKEY

Place of chaos

In the beginning God created the heavens and the earth. Now the earth was formless and empty, darkness was over the surface of the deep, and the Spirit of God was hovering over the waters. And God said, 'Let there be light,' and there was light. God saw that the light was good, and he separated the light from the darkness… And God said, 'Let the water teem with living creatures, and let birds fly above the earth across the vault of the sky.' So God created the great creatures of the sea and every living thing with which the water teems… And God saw that it was good.

At the very start of our scriptures, we are told how God takes that which is 'formless and empty' and brings order, making a world that is 'home' in ways as varied as its living creatures. It is part of the bold assertion of this story that creation is not a series of accidents or chance events, but the intentional and inspired work of an intelligent being.

There is no definitive answer as to who wrote Genesis, but most scholars believe it received its final form around the time of the Babylonian exile. During those years of turbulence and turmoil, God's people reminded themselves of their story of origins: the Spirit of God was present even in the darkness before creation took shape. At each point in the narrative, it is God who decides, shapes and decrees that the results are 'good'. Even 'the great creatures of the sea' (which some see as a possible reference to Tiamat, the Babylonian goddess of chaos) are called into being by God. And after each creative act, the pattern of night and day is another reminder that orderliness is fundamental to God's world.

When life is turned upside-down, when we feel threatened by the forces of chaos and disintegration, as did God's exiled people centuries before, we can remind ourselves of this very first story (whether we read it literally or figuratively). Echoing the Apostles' Creed, we can say: 'We believe in God, the Father almighty, creator of heaven and earth.'

What one thing can you do today to help safeguard the goodness of creation?

NAOMI STARKEY

Place of pride

As people moved eastward, they found a plain in Shinar and settled there. They said… 'Come, let us build ourselves a city, with a tower that reaches to the heavens, so that we may make a name for ourselves…' The Lord said, 'If as one people speaking the same language they have begun to do this, then nothing they plan to do will be impossible for them. Come, let us go down and confuse their language so they will not understand each other.' So the Lord scattered them from there over all the earth, and they stopped building the city.

It is hard to be certain of some of the details here, but Shinar has been identified with Babylonia, and the name given to the tower – Babel – sounds like the Hebrew for 'confused' but also Babylon, the empire that stood so proudly against God's people. There is speculation that the tower might have looked like the ziggurats of Near Eastern cities, massive brick platform structures sometimes topped by a temple.

The problem, as presented by this story, is not about architecture or the building of cities but the people's intent: uniting to 'make a name' for themselves by showing their reach is as high as the heavens. This is about power for its own sake, an attitude that says 'we know best'. Unity is not intrinsically wrong, but it can too easily slip into dominance by the loudest voices and strongest opinions. Power is not automatically bad, but wielding power, especially great power – imperial power – is fraught with difficulties, not least the temptation to hang on to power at all costs.

The confusion of language and scattering 'over all the earth' stopped the tower-building. It also established an important dynamic in social interaction: the need to work at understanding each other. Learning another language – whether another human language or a way of speaking involving a very different viewpoint from our own – is a humbling and sometimes fraught task. For that reason, it is one of the most useful things we can do.

Look for an opportunity today to 'listen' to a voice speaking a different 'language' to your own. What hopes and fears do you hear?

NAOMI STARKEY

Place of power

Marduk-Baladan son of Baladan king of Babylon sent Hezekiah letters and a gift… Hezekiah received the envoys and showed them all that was in his storehouses… Then Isaiah said to Hezekiah, 'Hear the word of the Lord: the time will surely come when everything in your palace, and all that your predecessors have stored up until this day, will be carried off to Babylon… And some of your descendants… will become eunuchs in the palace of the king of Babylon.' 'The word of the Lord you have spoken is good,' Hezekiah replied. For he thought, 'Will there not be peace and security in my lifetime?'

Of the generally sorry litany of kings in the Old Testament, Hezekiah is considered one of the better examples, reigning in Jerusalem over the kingdom of Judah in the late eighth and early seventh centuries BC. He forti-fied the city, ensuring a water supply in the event of a siege, and instituted wide-ranging religious reforms as well as managing to see off (with God's help) a planned conquest by Sennacherib, king of Assyria. During the same period, the neighbouring kingdom of Israel fell to Assyria and the people there were exiled to the homeland of their conquerors.

Eventually, however, Hezekiah's successes, as well as his undoubted faith in God, seem to have led him into a trap, as outlined in today's passage. Perhaps he felt invulnerable as he received the emissaries from Babylon, who had come ostensibly to congratulate him on his recovery from near-fatal illness. Even the prophet Isaiah's stern warning fails to drive home the foolishness of showing off the royal wealth to power-hungry visitors.

For so much of their history, Israel and Judah were overshadowed and at risk of being overwhelmed by neighbouring powers. Even a good king such as Hezekiah sometimes forgot a foundational truth about his royal authority: it came from God and could only be rightly exercised under God's guidance. Babylon did not represent a new kind of threat; sadly, Hezekiah's inadequate response was nothing new either, eventually undoing the posi-tive achievements of his earlier years.

Name in prayer government leaders, and ask for God's wisdom to prevail in their decision-making.

NAOMI STARKEY

Place of conquest

Nebuzaradan commander of the imperial guard, who served the king of Babylon, came to Jerusalem. He set fire to the temple of the Lord, the royal palace and all the houses of Jerusalem. Every important building he burned down. The whole Babylonian army, under the commander of the imperial guard, broke down all the walls around Jerusalem. Nebuzaradan… carried into exile some of the poorest people and those who remained in the city, along with the rest of the craftsmen and those who had deserted to the king of Babylon. But Nebuzaradan left behind the rest of the poorest people of the land to work the vineyards and fields.

Today's passage is part of a chapter that describes the fall of Jerusalem in devastating detail. The prophet Jeremiah had long foretold the likelihood of such an ending if the people did not heed his warnings. The comprehensive nature of the destruction ('temple… palace… all the houses… every important building') was surely beyond everyone's worst fears.

The end came after a siege of nearly two years. King Zedekiah had decided to rebel against the Babylonian king who had installed him on the throne. He ended up paying with his life as well as the lives of his sons and his civil servants, and the life of the kingdom as a whole. Apart from ruins, all that is left are enough labourers to harvest the land for the continued benefit of the conquerors. The book of Lamentations, traditionally credited to Jeremiah, expresses with poignant eloquence the ensuing tide of loss and mourning.

To the Babylonians, Judah was nothing special, just a small, annoying kingdom that had refused to toe the imperial line and so suffered the consequences. For Judah, this was not just about physical ruin; the whole of society was ripped apart, the covenant relationship with God apparently null and void. Mercifully, most of us will not have seen our homes and communities destroyed, yet that will have been the recent history of some countries no more than a plane-ride away.

Pray for the men, women and children who have to shape new lives from the ashes of what used to be.

NAOMI STARKEY

Place of lament

By the rivers of Babylon we sat and wept when we remembered Zion. There on the poplars we hung our harps, for there our captors asked us for songs, our tormentors demanded songs of joy; they said, 'Sing us one of the songs of Zion!' How can we sing the songs of the Lord while in a foreign land? If I forget you, Jerusalem, may my right hand forget its skill. May my tongue cling to the roof of my mouth if I do not remember you, if I do not consider Jerusalem my highest joy.

This lyrical psalm of lament evokes the landscape of exile and the deep anguish of the people forced to live there, far from everything they knew as home. Memories of what they have lost bring forth tears flowing as freely as the great rivers Euphrates and Tigris, which gave that whole region the name Mesopotamia ('land between rivers' in ancient Greek). Mighty those rivers may be, but they are not the Jordan, the river that marks entry into the promised land.

Despite their tears, the people's sorrow is compounded by their captors' demands for 'songs', expressions of joy when they feel unable to do anything except weep. To sing would be a betrayal of what they had lost, as if Jerusalem did not matter anymore. One of the struggles commonly experienced by the bereaved is the fear that forgetting their grief even for a moment is somehow disloyal to the one they are mourning.

As well as weeping, though, deep grief can be expressed in rage, and it is such rage that blazes out in the notorious final verses of this psalm, verses rarely (if ever) heard in public worship these days. The psalmist calls for the infants of Babylon to be brutally killed, the implication being that such treatment had been meted out to the babies of Judah. While the violent imagery is too disturbing to be recited without comment or explanation, we should not lose sight of the fact that, as a whole, the psalms show that anger, as much as praise, have an important part to play in prayer.

How easy do you find expressing your anger to God?

NAOMI STARKEY

Place of exile

Then the king ordered Ashpenaz, chief of his court officials, to bring into the king's service some of the Israelites from the royal family and the nobility... They were to be trained for three years, and after that they were to enter the king's service. Among those who were chosen were some from Judah: Daniel, Hananiah, Mishael and Azariah. The chief official gave them new names: to Daniel, the name Belteshazzar; to Hananiah, Shadrach; to Mishael, Meshach; and to Azariah, Abednego... To these four young men God gave knowledge and understanding of all kinds of literature and learning.

A few days ago, we had the sobering words of Isaiah, warning Hezekiah of the consequences of his foolish display of wealth: 'Some of your descendants... will become eunuchs in the palace of the king of Babylon.' We don't know whether Daniel and his companions were made eunuchs, although that was a common fate for young men taken into imperial service. We do know that they were treated as plunder, much as the treasures from the Jerusalem temple. Denied their former social status, they are even renamed: Daniel ('God is my judge') became Belteshazzar ('Bel [a Babylonian deity] protects his life').

Despite this context of exile, we hear of God's presence and blessing on Daniel and his friends. They had instigated an act of resistance, refusing to 'defile' themselves with the royal food and wine served as part of their training as king's staff. Miraculously, they suffer no ill effects and also prove to be gifted beyond their peers, even though these gifts will be used to benefit the empire that destroyed their homeland.

For God's people, Babylon meant exile from culture, community and, worst of all, the temple, which represented God's presence among them. What the years in Babylon would show is that the reach of the Lord of creation is not limited by space or time – or indeed exile.

'If I rise on the wings of the dawn, if I settle on the far side of the sea, even there your hand will guide me, your right hand will hold me fast'
(Psalm 139:9–10).

NAOMI STARKEY

Place of persecution

Nebuchadnezzar said to them, 'Is it true, Shadrach, Meshach and Abed-nego, that you do not serve my gods or worship the image of gold I have set up?... If you do not worship it, you will be thrown immediately into a blazing furnace. Then what god will be able to rescue you from my hand?' [They replied], 'King Nebuchadnezzar, we do not need to defend ourselves before you in this matter. If we are thrown into the blazing furnace, the God we serve is able to deliver us... But even if he does not, we want you to know, Your Majesty, that we will not serve your gods.'

Yesterday we reflected on the reassurance of God's presence no matter how far from home we are. Today we have a stark reminder of the vulnerability of living in a place of exile. Daniel's friends Hananiah, Mishael and Azariah (Shadrach, Meshach and Abednego) were prized members of the imperial civil service ('set over the affairs of the province of Babylon', v. 12), but that did not save them from being denounced as disloyal to the regime when Nebuchadnezzar instituted his new cult.

The story is told to full dramatic effect in Daniel 3, concluding in a miraculous deliverance. One who looked like 'a son of the gods' (v. 25) walked with them in the terrible furnace, so that the fire did not even singe their hair or scorch their clothes. This vindication of their faith shakes Nebuchadnezzar's arrogance to the extent that he hails them as 'servants of the Most High God' (v. 26).

We should note that the faith of the three friends is resolute even when the outcome is by no means certain. They were prepared to go along with new names and a new way of life – but they would not worship a new god, even if it cost them everything. In the end, they were not only delivered from death but honoured by the very king who tried to destroy them.

---

*'If we live, we live for the Lord; and if we die, we die for the Lord.
So, whether we live or die, we belong to the Lord' (Romans 14:8).*

NAOMI STARKEY

Place of downfall

As the king was walking on the roof of the royal palace of Babylon, he said, 'Is not this the great Babylon I have built as the royal residence, by my mighty power and for the glory of my majesty?'… A voice came from heaven, 'This is what is decreed for you, King Nebuchadnezzar: your royal authority has been taken from you. You will be driven away from people and will live with the wild animals; you will eat grass like the ox. Seven times will pass by for you until you acknowledge that the Most High is sovereign over all kingdoms on earth.'

While only the book of Daniel includes this shocking episode, Nebuchadnezzar (the second ruler of that name, c. 605–561BC) is well-documented as the greatest king of Babylon. A brilliant military strategist and diplomat, he also lavished attention on rebuilding and enhancing the city of Babylon, including the Ishtar Gate (now reconstructed in a Berlin museum) and the legendary Hanging Gardens (of which no trace remains). Well might such a figure stroll his flat palace rooftop, perhaps in the cool of the day, and survey his domain with enormous satisfaction.

Daniel 4 tells the full story, beginning with the king's dream of a great tree being cut down, which Daniel, deeply alarmed, interprets as foretelling humiliation and downfall for the king unless he acknowledges the power of the 'Most High' (v. 25). This warning is ignored and, a year later, events come to pass as foretold. Nebuchadnezzar suffers what sounds like some kind of breakdown and is restored to his right mind only after he 'raised his eyes towards heaven' (v. 34).

Just as intelligence has to mature to produce wisdom, so power has to be rightly exercised to avoid tyranny. Learning to balance justice with mercy, pride with humility and authority with mutuality are hugely challenging lessons. Nebuchadnezzar's (temporary) downfall shows that no human throne is beyond toppling; no human power base is eternal.

'He has shown you, O mortal, what is good. And what does the Lord require of you? To act justly and to love mercy and to walk humbly with your God'
(Micah 6:8).

NAOMI STARKEY

Place of encounter

I saw a violent storm coming out of the north – an immense cloud with flashing lightning and surrounded by brilliant light. The centre of the fire looked like glowing metal, and in the fire was what looked like four living creatures... Above the vault over their heads was what looked like a throne of lapis lazuli, and high above on the throne was a figure like that of a man... Like the appearance of a rainbow in the clouds on a rainy day, so was the radiance around him. This was the appearance of the likeness of the glory of the Lord.

This astonishing vision ('theophany' is the technical term) is precisely dated: it happens on the fifth day of the fourth month in the fifth year of the long exile in Babylon of King Jehoiachin of Judah. On the banks of the River Kebar, a 30-year-old Jewish priest, Ezekiel, sees 'the likeness of the glory of the Lord'. And so begins his prophetic ministry.

Ezekiel's visions can be almost hallucinogenic in their intensity (fiery living creatures in this first chapter) or downright terrifying (the valley of dry bones in Ezekiel 37, for example). His oracles can be shockingly graphic (such as the description of Jerusalem as an adulterous wife in Ezekiel 16). Sometimes God tells him to act out his message, literally embodying the people's suffering by lying on his side for 430 days. It is perhaps unsurprising that we find many echoes of Ezekiel in the book of Revelation, another part of scripture that calls for careful interpretation.

This prophetic energy and passion (not to say rage) burns fiercely despite the context of exile and loss of everything that meant 'home' for God's people. They might feel cast off, but Ezekiel's message is that God has not given up on them, despite their waywardness. In the end, dry bones will be restored, the temple rebuilt and meanwhile, for those with eyes to see, God's glory shines as brightly by a Babylonian waterway as in the Holy of Holies itself (see Isaiah 6).

'Holy, holy, holy is the Lord Almighty; the whole earth is full of his glory'
(Isaiah 6:3).

NAOMI STARKEY

Place of humiliation

'Go down, sit in the dust, Virgin Daughter Babylon; sit on the ground without a throne, queen city of the Babylonians. No more will you be called tender or delicate. Take millstones and grind flour; take off your veil. Lift up your skirts, bare your legs, and wade through the streams. Your nakedness will be exposed and your shame uncovered. I will take vengeance; I will spare no one.' Our Redeemer – the Lord Almighty is his name – is the Holy One of Israel… You said, 'I am forever – the eternal queen!' But you did not consider these things or reflect on what might happen.

At last the tables are turned: instead of Jerusalem humiliated in the dust, it is the turn of the 'queen city'. There is a note of glee in the description of her downfall: the fine lady forced to labour in the sun like any peasant girl.

Such mocking language makes for uncomfortable reading, especially when balanced against Jesus' injunction to 'love your enemies and pray for those who persecute you' (Matthew 5:44). We have to remember that Isaiah's words are not about denigrating women – or manual labour – in general. The prophet is sending a clear message that no human authority, however absolute it may seem, can endure forever unchallenged.

It is surprising to realise that even though God gave his people into Babylon's hands, Babylon is held to account for not showing them mercy (v. 6). Other nations, those not included in the covenant, are still called to abide by covenant standards of behaviour. This reminds us how the biblical view is that all power, without exception, comes from the hand of the Lord Almighty. If power is used cruelly and unjustly, good outcomes are unlikely to result, as is clear from the history of tyrants and bullies at every level of society, as well as in the teaching of scripture.

Babylon's fault lay not in being a 'queen city', but in being arrogant, cruel and complacent. Great power (and similarly great wealth) brings with it daunting responsibilities and demands, including the dangerous temptation to cling on to power at all costs.

'There's a wideness in God's mercy like the wideness of the sea'
(F.W. Faber, 1814–63).

NAOMI STARKEY

Place of corruption

I saw a woman sitting on a scarlet beast that was covered with blasphemous names and had seven heads and ten horns. The woman was dressed in purple and scarlet, and was glittering with gold, precious stones and pearls. She held a golden cup in her hand, filled with abominable things and the filth of her adulteries. The name written on her forehead was a mystery: BABYLON THE GREAT THE MOTHER OF PROSTITUTES AND OF THE ABOMINATIONS OF THE EARTH. I saw that the woman was drunk with the blood of God's holy people, the blood of those who bore testimony to Jesus.

The graphic imagery of yesterday's Bible passage is amplified in these verses from Revelation. At first glance, this reads like an unhelpful stereotype of the 'wicked temptress': 'woman… scarlet… glittering… prostitutes', hedged around by warnings of 'filth' and 'abominable things'. Over the centuries, condemnation rather than compassion has often characterised church attitudes towards women who have been judged as breaching moral codes. Recall, however, that the religious establishment condemned Jesus for associating with lepers and prostitutes, 'tax collectors and sinners'.

The point of the Babylon described here is to draw together themes reverberating throughout scripture into a symbol of all that stands defiantly against God. The lavish clothing and glittering wealth establish Babylon as an icon of bombastic power. The city covertly referenced here was Rome, centre of the greatest empire yet seen, with a succession of rulers worshipped as divine.

What is particularly notable is the emphasis on love betrayed or sold like any other commodity: Babylon has had multiple affairs and is the 'mother of prostitutes'. The Old Testament prophets returned repeatedly to language of marital infidelity to explore the anguished dynamic between the kingdoms of Israel and Judah and their Lord God. Faithful covenant relationship was overturned in favour of risky local alliances that apparently offered better economic and political security. In the end, such alliances came at a terrible price: that of destruction and exile.

Read Hosea chapters 1—3 for a moving story of love betrayed
but finally restored.

NAOMI STARKEY

Place of judgement

Then a mighty angel picked up a boulder the size of a large millstone and threw it into the sea, and said: 'With such violence the great city of Babylon will be thrown down, never to be found again. The music of harpists and musicians, pipers and trumpeters, will never be heard in you again. No worker of any trade will ever be found in you again… The light of a lamp will never shine in you again. The voice of bridegroom and bride will never be heard in you again… By your magic spell all the nations were led astray.'

Revelation, one of the most mysterious books in the Bible, declares that despite the turmoil of history, God is on the throne (4:2). Earthly thrones and dominions don't stand a chance, despite appearances to the contrary. Even the mighty Babylon (standing here, as yesterday, for Rome) will eventually be cast down. The same destruction meted out to conquered nations will be inflicted on that 'great city'. As was the fate of Judah long ago, so now the streets of Babylon will be emptied – no trading bustle, no community celebration, no family life.

The language of judgement sits uncomfortably with us these days and rightly so, for in times past Christians have been swift to pass judgement on others. The wider context of Revelation shows that the judgement on Babylon is about protecting others from harm, rather than wreaking savage vengeance for its own sake. A society – and an economic system – rooted in corruption and cruelty is decisively ended. No more innocent blood will be spilled.

We also have to balance the fierce energy of today's verses with what the Bible tells of God's longing to show mercy, even before repentance has happened. The loving father in Jesus' parable came running to forgive his runaway son even though he was 'still a long way off' (Luke 15:20).

'Seek the Lord while he may be found; call on him while he is near.
Let the wicked forsake their ways and the unrighteous their thoughts.
Let them turn to the Lord, and he will have mercy on them, and to our God,
for he will freely pardon' (Isaiah 55:6–7).

NAOMI STARKEY

Place of sojourn

Paul, a servant of Christ Jesus, called to be an apostle and set apart for the gospel of God… regarding his Son, who as to his earthly life was a descendant of David, and who through the Spirit of holiness was appointed the Son of God in power by his resurrection from the dead: Jesus Christ our Lord. Through him we received grace and apostleship to call all the Gentiles to the obedience that comes from faith for his name's sake… To all in Rome who are loved by God and called to be his holy people.

Nebuchadnezzar's Babylon, at one time the largest city in the world, is now a mound of broken clay bricks near Baghdad. Rome ceased to be an imperial city in the fifth century AD. While superpowers remain a feature of world affairs today, individual political freedom is arguably more wide-spread than ever. At the same time, the dominance of market-driven economics has led to enormous wealth for some but corresponding inequality for many. Meanwhile, Babylon still stands for oppression for disciples of Rastafarianism, who equate it in part with the colonial history and capitalist agendas that led to so many non-white groups living in poverty.

Writing to the new Christians in the Babylon of his day, Paul reminds them of their calling to be God's 'holy people', committed to a different kingdom 'not of this world' (see John 18:36). That did not mean fleeing the unholy city, but being ready to pay the price of allegiance to the Most High God rather than to a human emperor, however godlike his status.

Following in their footsteps, we face a similar challenge of being sojourners in a world that can sometimes feel as alienating as those earlier Babylons. We may not face overt persecution or death threats, but, like the earliest believers, we need Christ-given grace to develop and maintain a kingdom-shaped perspective on our lives, our values and our choices. Thanks be to God that, as Paul reminds us, this grace is just part of what we receive through Jesus' death and resurrection.

'For the Lion of Judah shall break every chain, and give us the victory, again and again' (Henry Wilson, 1828–78).

NAOMI STARKEY

Place of blessing

Rejoice in the Lord always. I will say it again: rejoice! Let your gentleness be evident to all. The Lord is near. Do not be anxious about anything, but in every situation, by prayer and petition, with thanksgiving, present your requests to God. And the peace of God, which transcends all understanding, will guard your hearts and your minds in Christ Jesus. Finally, brothers and sisters, whatever is true, whatever is noble, whatever is right, whatever is pure, whatever is lovely, whatever is admirable – if anything is excellent or praiseworthy – think about such things.

The letter to the church in Philippi is one of the so-called 'captivity epistles'. Along with Ephesians, Colossians and Philemon, it is traditionally believed to have been written when Paul was a prisoner in Rome. Philippi was only a medium-sized city, but as a Roman colony in Macedonia it had close ties to the imperial metropolis. The people would have been proud of their status as Roman citizens, but Paul reminds them in his letter of the importance of cherishing their commitment to another, greater principality – the kingdom of heaven.

The way of God's kingdom involves imitating Christ's servant-like humility, rather than relishing privilege. It means living in such a way that they shine like stars in the midst of the dark and corrupt world around them. Above all, it means holding fast to the salvation won on the cross, rather than being led astray by any other teaching.

As the letter concludes, Paul bursts out in the lyrical exhortation above, urging holy thoughts, heavenly joy and transcendent peace that is within the grasp of every believer. Speaking from his prison cell, he shows that life can be more than survival, even in the very heart of the contemporary Babylon, as well as in its outlying realms. Despite potential or actual threats to body and soul, the followers of the Way (as the early Christians were described) can enjoy blessing beyond expectation, safe in the knowledge that 'the Lord is near' – even in Babylon.

'Blessings abound where'er he reigns, the prisoner leaps to lose his chains; the weary find eternal rest, and all the sons of want are blest'
(Isaac Watts, 1674–1748).

NAOMI STARKEY

Desert spirituality

From the third century after Christ, some Christians sought to live in a more disciplined manner by adopting a life of poverty, simplicity and celibacy, at first within the Mediterranean cities but gradually moving towards solitude in the desert, especially in Egypt. Once Christianity was legalised in the early fourth century and moved towards becoming the state religion, this practice grew, as Christians grew uncomfortable with the compromises the church was making with general society, and wanted to live their faith in a more dedicated way: as hermits, perhaps with a few disciples living near them, or sometimes in monasteries where they could be trained in holiness. These ascetics came to be known as the desert fathers (though there were quite a few desert mothers too).

In his book *The Way of the Heart* (Seabury Press, 1981), Henri Nouwen characterises the core practices of the desert fathers as solitude, silence and constant prayer. They avoided company, fasted often, ate little, dressed simply and aimed to focus entirely on God. To finance their simple lifestyle they undertook manual work, often plaiting palm leaves to make ropes or baskets. They also, like most desert dwellers, set great store by hospitality and would sometimes eat with a guest even though they were meant to be fasting, simply to express fellowship.

Benedicta Ward, who collected the sayings of these monks and nuns in *The Desert Fathers* (Penguin, 2003), identifies other characteristics of their life as self-control, fortitude, sober living, doing nothing for show, non-judgement of others, discretion, humility, obedience, patience and charity. They sought God by fleeing the world, rather than seeing God in the world.

We may find their lifestyle extreme and some of their sayings eccentric, but there is much wisdom in their pithy statements born of experience. Even if we do not adopt their solitary life today, we can still learn from their renunciation of comfort in order to seek God.

I have chosen in these notes to bring their tradition together with the various meanings of the desert or wilderness in the Bible (the two terms are fairly interchangeable). Most of the notes end with a provocative or inspiring saying from the fathers or mothers, to stimulate our reflection and prayer.

VERONICA ZUNDEL

Unchosen wilderness

So Abraham rose early in the morning, and took bread and a skin of water, and gave it to Hagar... along with the child, and sent her away. And she departed, and wandered about in the wilderness of Beer-sheba. When the water in the skin was gone, she cast the child under one of the bushes. Then she went and sat down opposite him a good way off... for she said, 'Do not let me look on the death of the child.' And as she sat opposite him, she lifted up her voice and wept. And God heard the voice of the boy; and the angel of God called to Hagar from heaven, and said to her, 'What troubles you, Hagar? Do not be afraid; for God has heard the voice of the boy where he is...' Then God opened her eyes, and she saw a well of water. She went, and filled the skin with water, and gave the boy a drink. God was with the boy, and he grew up; he lived in the wilderness, and became an expert with the bow.

Often when we speak of being in a spiritual desert, it is something we have not chosen for ourselves. Perhaps some tragedy has happened or we have just grown weary of everyday life. As I write, we are nearing the end of the Covid-19 lockdown and the isolation has felt like a desert to many.

Hagar, mother of the son Abraham fathered when he was tired of waiting for God's promise to be fulfilled, has been thrown out now that Sarah, his wife, has had Isaac. She is homeless, workless and with no means to support her child. It is like the situation my Polish birth grandmother faced, fleeing pogroms in World War I, arriving in Vienna having lost track of her husband, with four children and pregnant with my mother.

Yet even the unchosen wilderness can be a place of vision and provision. In an earlier exile (Genesis 16:7–14), Hagar has already heard the voice of God and been the first person to give God a name: 'You are El-roi' (16:13) – that is, 'God who sees'.

'You count my wanderings. You put my tears into your container. Aren't they in your book?' (Psalm 56:8, WEB).

VERONICA ZUNDEL

Lost and found

He divided the sea and let them pass through it, and made the waters stand like a heap. In the daytime he led them with a cloud, and all night long with a fiery light. He split rocks open in the wilderness, and gave them drink abundantly as from the deep. He made streams come out of the rock, and caused waters to flow down like rivers. Yet they sinned still more against him, rebelling against the Most High in the desert. They tested God in their heart by demanding the food they craved. They spoke against God, saying, 'Can God spread a table in the wilderness?'

Every year in the Passover meal, observant Jews retell the story of how God freed their ancestors from slavery in Egypt. Prominent in this story is the 40 years the children of Israel wandered in the desert, unable to make progress because they repeatedly turned away from God.

Biblically, the desert is often portrayed as a place of lostness. The desert fathers and mothers could also experience this sense of futility, as they struggled with their own thoughts and sought to become more Christlike. But they had chosen desert life for exactly this purpose: not to escape from God's call but to confront their own sinfulness and to grow in godliness. They were often tempted to a more comfortable life, and some indeed returned to 'the world', giving up on their solitary life.

The movement towards monastic life, especially the hermit life, was a particular phase in the history of the church, and few seem to be called to it today. But we all still need to be alone with God, to examine ourselves and be brought face to face with our flaws – not to punish us, but to make us humble and ready to be changed into the likeness of Christ (see 2 Corinthians 3:18). We may do this through quiet days or retreats, or simply by making time for prayer at home. When we do, we will discover not only our own frailty, but how much God loves us.

Antony said, 'He who sits alone and is quiet has escaped from three wars: hearing, speaking, seeing; but there is one thing against he must continually fight: that is, his own heart.'

VERONICA ZUNDEL

A place of provision

When the Most High apportioned the nations, when he divided human-kind, he fixed the boundaries of the peoples according to the number of the gods; the Lord's own portion was his people, Jacob his allotted share. He sustained him in a desert land, in a howling wilderness waste; he shielded him, cared for him, guarded him as the apple of his eye. As an eagle stirs up its nest, and hovers over its young; as it spreads its wings, takes them up, and bears them aloft on its pinions, the Lord alone guided him; no foreign god was with him.

Poverty and fasting were key practices for the desert fathers and mothers. They wanted to discipline their physical desires, to focus on the spiritual. Yet they also often experienced God's miraculous provision. Take this story from the sayings of the desert fathers.

Someone brought a hermit who was a leper some money and said, 'Take this to spend, for you are old and ill.' He replied, 'Are you going to take me away from Him who has fed me for 60 years? I have been ill all that time, and have needed nothing because God has fed me and given me what I need.' He would not accept it.

We need not go to the extremes of poverty such Christians embraced to find that when we can't provide for ourselves, God will provide for us – whether our needs be for food, human contact or the resources to answer a particular calling. Sometimes the provision is 'just enough' to keep us going; sometimes it is beyond our wildest expectations. After all, Jesus promised, 'I came that they may have life, and have it abundantly' (John 10:10).

In today's passage, the phrase 'according to the number of the gods' suggests that it is of very early origin, when God's people thought God provided only for them. Later, they would grow to know their God is God of all and provides for all who choose to follow.

When asked if absolute poverty was absolute goodness, Syncletica replied, 'It is a great good for those who can do it… As strong clothes are laundered pure white by being turned and trodden underfoot in water, a strong soul is strengthened by freely accepting poverty.'

VERONICA ZUNDEL

Wanton cravings

Our ancestors, when they were in Egypt, did not consider your wonderful works; they did not remember the abundance of your steadfast love, but rebelled against the Most High at the Red Sea. Yet he saved them for his name's sake… He rebuked the Red Sea, and it became dry; he led them through the deep as through a desert. So he saved them from the hand of the foe, and delivered them from the hand of the enemy… But they soon forgot his works… they had a wanton craving in the wilderness, and put God to the test in the desert; he gave them what they asked, but sent a wasting disease among them.

In the sayings of the desert fathers, one of the longest themed chapters is 'Lust'. Those who retreated to the desert chose celibacy, but it was not an easy choice. Both male and female monastics battled daily with wayward desires and fantasies, not just for sex but for more food, luxuries and all the comforts of a 'normal' life. Some had visions of demons whom they had to repel with prayer.

Reading these ancient texts, we may find the men's attitudes to women strange, even insulting: one even refused to see his mother because she was a woman. We may suspect they failed to see the difference between lust and healthy, natural desire. We may also think of Paul's advice that 'it is better to marry than to be aflame with passion' (1 Corinthians 7:9), and wonder why these people subjected themselves to such strictures. But their calling was to focus their lives only on God, and they saw marriage and family as a distraction. Some Christians still have a calling to celibacy, and we should support them with deep friendship and care.

We have our own 'wanton cravings' – for fame, wealth or anything else we feel is missing in our lives. Sometimes, as in today's passage, God will give us what we want, but it may be a disappointment! God alone is our true food (John 4:32).

They said of Sarah that for 13 years she was fiercely attacked by the demon of lust. She never prayed that the battle should leave her, but she used to say only, 'Lord, give me strength.'

VERONICA ZUNDEL

Down but not out

Ahab told Jezebel all that Elijah had done, and how he had killed all the prophets with the sword. Then Jezebel sent a messenger to Elijah, saying, 'So may the gods do to me, and more also, if I do not make your life like the life of one of them by this time tomorrow.' Then he was afraid; he got up and fled for his life, and came to Beer-sheba, which belongs to Judah; he left his servant there. But he himself went a day's journey into the wilderness, and came and sat down under a solitary broom tree. He asked that he might die: 'It is enough; now, O Lord, take away my life, for I am no better than my ancestors.'

In my first term at university, I had an overwhelming spiritual experience which I still don't understand fully, nearly 50 years later. For days afterwards, my jaw literally ached from smiling so much! But soon after, I was plunged into what I now recognise as my first episode of depression.

We are all familiar with the phenomenon of a great high being followed by a deep low. Elijah has given his all to demonstrating that his God is real and the pagan gods are not. Now he is spiritually, emotionally and physically drained and afraid of repercussions from hostile authorities. The desert, physical or spiritual, can be a place of great fear: how will I survive? Will I give up? Forgetting his recent triumph, his dramatic encounter with God, Elijah succumbs to self-doubt and despair.

Solitary, often hungry or ill, battling with demons internal and external, the desert fathers and mothers were often discouraged and despondent. Apart from their own spiritual struggles, they may have had anxious family or friends urging them to give up this extreme way of life for the sake of their health. Some did, but most were determined to seek God through solitude, silence and prayer; and in the process many became spiritual giants, people of wisdom whom others sought out for counsel. Paul's 'thorn in the flesh' (2 Corinthians 12:7) kept him from being over-elated. Failure can sometimes teach us more than success can.

A hermit said, 'I would rather be defeated and humble than win and be proud.'

VERONICA ZUNDEL

A haunt of angels

Then he lay down under the broom tree and fell asleep. Suddenly an angel touched him and said to him, 'Get up and eat.' He looked, and there at his head was a cake baked on hot stones, and a jar of water. He ate and drank, and lay down again. The angel of the Lord came a second time, touched him, and said, 'Get up and eat, otherwise the journey will be too much for you.' He got up, and ate and drank; then he went in the strength of that food forty days and forty nights to Horeb the mount of God.

When I was 41, I had a rough time giving birth to my son, and after just one night back home, I was hauled back into hospital with an infection. Stuck in a side room on the gynaecology ward, I was on a double drip moored to the bed and trying to feed and change my baby.

Then the 'day of angels' came. They were human angels: midwives, nurses and health visitors. But each one brought me a blessing: a useful tip, an acknowledgement of what a hard time I had had. Those five days back in hospital were a desert, but a desert haunted by angels.

For Elijah, the desert may be a place of despair, but it is also a place of healing. If the desert was a place of demons for the desert fathers and mothers, it was also a place of angels, and often the angels were the monk's or nun's fellow hermits.

Jesus said, 'It is more blessed to give than to receive' (Acts 20:35), but he himself often received care and gifts from others, especially women (see, for example, Luke 8:1–3; Matthew 26:6–13). Receiving as well as giving keeps us humble and creates love between fellow disciples.

A brother asked a hermit, 'Suppose there are two monks: one stays quietly in his cell, fasting for six days at a time… and the other ministers to the sick. Which of them is more pleasing to God?' He replied, 'Even if the brother who fasts six days hung himself up by his nose, he wouldn't be the equal of him who ministers to the sick.'

VERONICA ZUNDEL

A place of preparation

A voice cries out: 'In the wilderness prepare the way of the Lord, make straight in the desert a highway for our God. Every valley shall be lifted up, and every mountain and hill be made low; the uneven ground shall become level, and the rough places a plain. Then the glory of the Lord shall be revealed, and all people shall see it together, for the mouth of the Lord has spoken.'

Being of Austrian parentage, and having visited the country since child-hood, I love mountains. So this prophecy of everything being levelled is not exactly enticing to me (I feel much the same about the vision in Revelation of there being no more sea – Revelation 21:1). But for the ancient Israelites, mountains were dangerous places, the hideout of bandits (see the parable of the Good Samaritan, Luke 10:30 – the Jericho road was a rocky, desert road), and the sea was unpredictable and killed many.

As I read this passage, I also hear the wonderful music of Handel's *Messiah*, and realise that it is about our journey being made safe. For those whose lives are full of tragedy or who experience dramatic mood swings, the idea of 'level ground' is reassuring (see Psalm 143:10, a favourite verse of mine).

The level ground is not just to make our lives easier. It is preparing a way for God to come among us. The Bible says little about our going to God when we die; instead it promises: 'See, the home of God is among mortals. He will dwell with them; they will be his peoples, and God himself will be with them' (Revelation 21:3). This was partly fulfilled in Jesus' incarnation, and it will be fully realised when he returns.

I find it interesting that God comes to us not in an impressive setting, but in the very wilderness where we may feel far from God. Deserts are places of absence, but they can also become places of presence.

Syncletica said, 'Sailors beginning a voyage set the sails and look for a favourable wind, and later they meet a contrary wind… They do not throw the cargo overboard or abandon ship; they wait a while and struggle against the storm until they can set a direct course again.'

VERONICA ZUNDEL

The desert of sin

The beginning of the good news of Jesus Christ, the Son of God. As it is written in the prophet Isaiah, 'See, I am sending my messenger ahead of you, who will prepare your way; the voice of one crying out in the wilderness: "Prepare the way of the Lord, make his paths straight"', John the baptiser appeared in the wilderness, proclaiming a baptism of repentance for the forgiveness of sins. And people from the whole Judean countryside and all the people of Jerusalem were going out to him, and were baptised by him in the river Jordan, confessing their sins. Now John was clothed with camel's hair, with a leather belt around his waist, and he ate locusts and wild honey.

The good news of Jesus starts in the wilderness, with a wild, austere man of the desert. Mark sees John the Baptist's appearing as a direct fulfilment of the prophecy we looked at yesterday. Why did Jesus need this forerunner? Partly because of such prophecies: the Jews expected the Messiah to be heralded by a new prophet, in the tradition of Elijah; at every Passover meal still, a seat is left empty for Elijah and at one point a child goes to open the door to see if he has come.

John himself denied being Elijah (John 1:21); Jesus, however, was more ready to give him the title (Matthew 11:13–14). Perhaps John wanted to focus more on his calling to make people aware of their own failings and to call them to righteousness. The journey towards faith in Jesus can take many forms, but a common one is to become convinced of one's sinfulness, one's emptiness without him. In some historic revivals, people wept for days for their sins before they reached a sense of God's forgiveness.

As I get older, my sense of being a sinner grows and sometimes it can feel as if I am in a desert of my own making. But the desert is where God clears the ground for a new shoot of redemption.

Mathois said, 'The nearer a man comes to God, the more he sees himself to be a sinner. Isaiah the prophet saw the Lord and knew himself to be wretched and unclean.'

VERONICA ZUNDEL

Beasts and angels

In those days Jesus came from Nazareth of Galilee and was baptised by John in the Jordan. And just as he was coming up out of the water, he saw the heavens torn apart and the Spirit descending like a dove on him. And a voice came from heaven, 'You are my Son, the Beloved; with you I am well pleased.' And the Spirit immediately drove him out into the wilderness. He was in the wilderness for forty days, tempted by Satan; and he was with the wild beasts; and the angels waited on him.

As with Elijah, so with Jesus. A major spiritual high is followed by a time of testing and loneliness. We expect a dramatic experience of the Holy Spirit to lead us into ever greater blessing and effectiveness, but it was the same Spirit who 'drove' Jesus into the wilderness. The Catholic writer Richard Rohr teaches that only suffering or loss can lead us from the first, immature stage of our lives, which is all about achieving, to maturity, where we are ready to let go of everything and rely utterly on God.

If you don't know them, look up Stanley Spencer's wonderful series of paintings *Christ in the Wilderness*. He shows an earthy, very human Jesus contemplating wildflowers, a hen and her chicks, little foxes, vultures and a scorpion, and praising or crying out to God. Thus he suggests that everything Jesus later fed into his parables originated in this time of contemplation and struggle. Spencer was himself going through isolation when he painted them.

In the desert Jesus encountered the worst and the best aspects of what it means to be human. If we are 'in Christ' by virtue of having given our lives to him, however incompletely or imperfectly, God says of us too, 'You are my child, the Beloved.' This doesn't mean we will always be protected or pampered. We may encounter our own deserts, but God will be with us in them. We may be surrounded by wild beasts, but there will also be angels.

Some hermits used to say, 'If you see a young man climbing up to heaven by his own will, catch him by the foot and pull him down to earth, for it is not good for him.'

VERONICA ZUNDEL

A place of testing

The tempter came and said to him, 'If you are the Son of God, command these stones to become loaves of bread.' But he answered, 'It is written, "One does not live by bread alone, but by every word that comes from the mouth of God."' Then the devil... placed him on the pinnacle of the temple, saying... 'If you are the Son of God, throw yourself down; for it is written... "On their hands they will bear you up, so that you will not dash your foot against a stone."' Jesus said to him, 'Again it is written, "Do not put the Lord your God to the test."' Again, the devil took him to a very high mountain and showed him all the kingdoms of the world... and he said... 'All these I will give you, if you will fall down and worship me.' Jesus said to him, 'Away with you, Satan! for it is written, "Worship the Lord your God, and serve only him."'

'Lead us not into temptation.' This line from the Lord's Prayer can also be translated 'Save us from the time of trial.' I prefer this version, because 'temptation' has acquired too many overtones: in advertising, 'tempting' has come to denote something we are encouraged to indulge in. Why would God 'lead' us there?

'Trial', however, suggests a test, something we might not have the strength to endure. From a difficult family situation to persecution of Christians (often by other Christians!), we are all likely to face some challenge that feels too hard and turn to God for strength.

Jesus' time of testing confronts him with three classic diversions: self-indulgence, doing things for show and exerting power over others. His response will set the whole tone of his ministry. By resisting, he shows that he will only perform miracles for the benefit of others, he will refuse to exploit his relationship to God for fame or acclaim, and he will lay down his power and become a servant.

'When [John] was dying... his brothers stood around him and asked for a sentence that would sum up the way to salvation... He said, "I have never obeyed my own will, and I never taught anyone to do anything which I did not do myself first."'

VERONICA ZUNDEL

A place of vision

Moses was keeping the flock of his father-in-law Jethro, the priest of Midian; he led his flock beyond the wilderness, and came to Horeb, the mountain of God. There the angel of the Lord appeared to him in a flame of fire out of a bush; he looked, and the bush was blazing, yet it was not consumed. Then Moses said, 'I must turn aside and look at this great sight, and see why the bush is not burned up.' When the Lord saw that he had turned aside to see, God called to him out of the bush, 'Moses, Moses!' And he said, 'Here I am.' Then he said, 'Come no closer! Remove the sandals from your feet, for the place on which you are standing is holy ground.'

As a child, when I had a row with my mother, I would run out of the house and walk to the nearby railway halt. I would climb the footbridge over the track and just gaze down the line. Somehow this longer view gave me a sense of perspective, calmed me and made me ready to go back and make peace.

Retreats may offer the same new view for those able to go on them. Even popping into a local church that is open during the day, lighting a candle or sitting in quiet can have this effect. For Moses, crossing the wilderness opens his eyes to the presence of God in the most unexpected places. He is just doing his daily work, leading sheep to safe pasture, and then everything changes.

The image of fire is a common one among the accounts left by the desert mystics. Their life of constant prayer sometimes (but not every day) issued in an all-consuming passion for God, like a fire burning in their hearts and bodies. The Bible too describes God as a 'consuming fire' (Hebrews 12:29) – not a fire which consumes our individuality, but one that purges us of faults (see Malachi 3:2–3).

A brother went to the cell of Arsenius in Scetis, and looked in through the window, and saw him like fire from head to foot… When he knocked, Arsenius came out and… said to him, 'Have you been knocking long? Did you see anything?' He answered, 'No.'

VERONICA ZUNDEL

A place of healing

Therefore, I will now persuade her, and bring her into the wilderness, and speak tenderly to her. From there I will give her her vineyards, and make the Valley of Achor a door of hope. There she shall respond as in the days of her youth, as at the time when she came out of the land of Egypt… I will make for you a covenant on that day with the wild animals, the birds of the air, and the creeping things of the ground; and I will abolish the bow, the sword, and war from the land; and I will make you lie down in safety.

Hosea was called by God to marry a prostitute, who would symbolise the unfaithfulness of Israel to God. But as early as chapter 2, after a long passage of condemnation of God's faithless people, the prophet turns to words of restoration and healing. This healing begins with the wife/Israel being brought into the wilderness. The wilderness may seem a strange place to find new life, but there God promises fruitful vineyards, an end to trouble ('Achor' means 'trouble') and a new relationship with creation and humanity.

This restoration includes both harmony with wild creatures and an end to war and weapons of war. When we talk of salvation and all it means, do we include these promises in our preaching or witness? Our faith is meant to inspire us to care better for God's creation and to make peace, not war. It is not just about rescuing individuals, but redeeming society and the planet.

The desert fathers and mothers may have been fleeing from society and everyday life, from the corruption of power and the danger of comfortable complacency. However, I'm sure their prayers were not just for themselves and their fellow monks and nuns, but also for the society they had left. Certainly those few who choose a hermit life today, benefit us all by their life of prayer.

When Ephraim of holy memory was a boy, he saw in sleep… that a vine was planted on his tongue and it grew and filled the whole earth with very great fruitfulness, and so all the birds of the air came and ate the fruits of that vine and spread the fruit further.

VERONICA ZUNDEL

A place of sharing

Then an angel of the Lord said to Philip, 'Get up and go towards the south to the road that goes down from Jerusalem to Gaza.' (This is a wilderness road.) So he got up and went. Now there was an Ethiopian eunuch, a court official of the Candace, queen of the Ethiopians, in charge of her entire treasury. He had come to Jerusalem to worship and was returning home; seated in his chariot, he was reading the prophet Isaiah. Then the Spirit said to Philip, 'Go over to this chariot and join it.' So Philip ran up to it and heard him reading the prophet Isaiah. He asked, 'Do you understand what you are reading?' He replied, 'How can I, unless someone guides me?' And he invited Philip to get in and sit beside him.

Do you ever wonder what your legacy will be? There are your children, if you have any, and perhaps a charity donation in your will, but what else? The latter part of this story tells us the eunuch was reading Isaiah 53, one of the 'servant songs', and perhaps this story of a mysterious man with no physical heirs spoke to his own situation. He may have been castrated from birth, which gave him a high position in the Ethiopian hierarchy (as he would be trusted among the royal women), but it deprived him of marriage and children.

Yet with Philip's explanation that this passage points to Jesus – another childless man – he learns that he is important to God, that he can have 'faith offspring' by sharing the Jesus story. For one of my poetry MA assignments, I wrote a dramatic monologue by this man, ending with the line, 'Oh, the faith-children I'll have, when I tell them this news.' Now he had been baptised, he had a new legacy, one of faith. No wonder he 'went on his way rejoicing' (v. 39).

Those who chose the desert life were celibate (and the men were discouraged from meeting with women, or even having young boys living with them). But the more experienced had disciples, and their wise, pithy sayings, written down by their followers, are still read today more than 1,500 years later.

Hyperichius said, 'He who teaches others by his life and not his speech is truly wise.'

VERONICA ZUNDEL

From desert to fertile ground

The wilderness and the dry land shall be glad, the desert shall rejoice and blossom; like the crocus it shall blossom abundantly, and rejoice with joy and singing… Then the eyes of the blind shall be opened, and the ears of the deaf unstopped; then the lame shall leap like a deer, and the tongue of the speechless sing for joy. For waters shall break forth in the wilderness, and streams in the desert; the burning sand shall become a pool, and the thirsty ground springs of water; the haunt of jackals shall become a swamp, the grass shall become reeds and rushes.

From the west coast to the east coast of the broadest part of Africa, south of the Sahara, more than 20 countries and as many development bodies are creating the Great Green Wall. This is an area of reforestation and environmental restoration that will hold back desertification, reduce carbon emissions and bring food security to millions.

The idea of 'greening' the desert is not new. Thousands of years ago, Isaiah pictured the desert being transformed into lush, well-watered, productive land. This is not just a promise of spiritual fertility, but of real physical transformation of the world we know. The 'new Jerusalem' picture in Revelation 21 is a garden city, with a broad river running through it, bordered by fruitful trees whose very leaves are a source of healing.

As an article I read recently about the sacraments put it, 'God works through stuff.' If matter didn't matter, would God have made so much of it? The desert fathers lived lives of great austerity and self-denial. We may think they were turning their backs on the material world. However, they did so not only to destroy their worst impulses, but also in the hope of the restoration of all things in the kingdom of God. Hyperichius told his disciples, 'Follow the gentleness of Moses, and hollow out the rocky places of your heart, so that you turn them into springs of water.'

'Therefore do not worry, saying, "What will we eat?" or "What will we drink?" or "What will we wear?"… But strive first for the kingdom of God and his righteousness, and all these things will be given to you as well'
(Matthew 6:31, 33).

VERONICA ZUNDEL

The parables of Jesus

'I will open my mouth to speak in parables; I will proclaim what has been hidden from the foundation of the world.'
MATTHEW 13:35 (NRSV)

Jesus told many stories. Unlike argument, which encourages taking a position or defending an existing view, stories simply 'are'. They invite us in. They enter the imagination, are held in memory and open their meanings over time, as we are ready. They are well-suited to reveal deep wisdom of life and heart.

Over the next fortnight, we'll be looking at a few stories from Luke's gospel. They are parables of relationship: love of neighbour and God's love for us. They all challenged the religious leaders of the day.

We begin with the good Samaritan. We meet a lawyer deep in the tradition of intellectual debate. By answering him with a story, Jesus encourages him to respond with empathy and action. The context of their exchange is illuminating. Seventy disciples have just returned from mission. Jesus is listening as they report lives transformed. They tell of action to help people, moved by the Spirit. He rejoices that these things are hidden from the wise and revealed to infants. 'Just then' the lawyer stands up and asks his questions, and the story unfolds. Luke balances all this talk of action with the story of Martha and Mary, where Mary sits at Jesus' feet, listening as a disciple. Both are important.

The second week is devoted to three parables of lost things. Here too the setting is important. In the previous chapter, Jesus is eating at a Pharisee's house where he speaks of the kingdom as a feast. Then, he is surrounded by those described as 'tax collectors and sinners'. He welcomes them and eats with them. I believe that as they eat together, these stories are told. In each story, God's joy is revealed by feasting and celebrating.

All look deep into the human heart, encouraging us to examine our motives and our actions. They help us know the love of God and what it means to love our neighbour and brother. All invite us to join our lives with the great prayer, 'May thy kingdom come on earth as in heaven.'

May their slow revelation offer us light to live by.

ANDREA SKEVINGTON

Debate and lived experience

At that same hour Jesus rejoiced in the Holy Spirit and said, 'I thank you, Father, Lord of heaven and earth, because you have hidden these things from the wise and the intelligent and have revealed them to infants... Just then a lawyer stood up to test Jesus. 'Teacher,' he said, 'what must I do to inherit eternal life?' He said to him, 'What is written in the law? What do you read there?'

We begin with an interruption, one that reveals two different ways of living a life of faith. Jesus is full of joy at how God's love transforms lives, of the kingdom coming on earth as it is in heaven. Then a lawyer stands up seeking an intellectual debate about salvation, rather than noticing this good news here and now. He may be hoping for a satisfying game of theology tennis – back and forth – but such games do nothing to touch the heart and transform the life.

The life of faith can become dry. It can become a pursuit of correct doctrine only and can lose the very life it seeks. Take a pause to reflect on times when churches you know have overflowed with God's love in a practical way and when they may have become absorbed in argument, looking in. I can remember when a church I was part of showed much love: gave small gifts to people in the street, helped the housebound or prayed with people outside. Such things may seem very small miracles, but they were part of an outflow of life.

Jesus' response to the lawyer is respectful, but Jesus does not join the game. He does not use force of will or mind. He is not concerned with winning, or even having, an argument. Perhaps there is a lesson here for us when we are tempted to join in debates on social media or argue people into right thinking. Jesus was giving his attention to the kingdom work of goodness and healing and hope. Perhaps we can, too, grounded in a deeper wisdom of the way of love.

'Does not wisdom call, and does not understanding raise her voice? On the heights, beside the way, at the crossroads she takes her stand... O simple ones, learn prudence' (Proverbs 8:1–2, 5).

ANDREA SKEVINGTON

Do we put limits on love?

[The lawyer] answered, 'You shall love the Lord your God with all your heart, and with all your soul, and with all your strength, and with all your mind; and your neighbour as yourself.' And [Jesus] said to him, 'You have given the right answer; do this, and you will live.' But wanting to justify himself, he asked Jesus, 'And who is my neighbour?'

We give time to this question of who is our neighbour. Maybe as we go deeper with these verses, we can allow it to open our eyes and hearts. The lawyer knows the way to life is love. However, his self-justification reveals love as rote-learned knowledge, rather than heart's wisdom. Being right doesn't help him love. Quibbling over love shrivels it up.

So what does loving our neighbour look like? Jesus will show us as we move through the story. Within it, we will see a practice we can work on. For now, let's turn again to 'And who is my neighbour?'

At this point, it looks like the reason for the lawyer's question is to limit his circle of compassion, to find out who must be included and who can be excluded. Such constraints on love seem against its very nature, but so often we do exclude. We reach the limits of our love. We may be short of time, energy and resources. Love may take us to very difficult places, and we hold back. We may have categories of people we overlook. The story to come will stretch our circle to love more widely. But it is a big stretch. I believe we can take time with this work and learn wisdom alongside love.

I learned much about the practice of loving my neighbour by becoming friends with a homeless young woman in our small town. Unlike the man in the story to come, her wounds were unseen. I found that I had to set aside my solutions to her problems and respectfully listen and learn from her. In time, she found a flat and work and community. I believe compassionate listening helped her take those steps for herself.

May we expand our circle of compassion and see neighbours everywhere.
May we live today from a grounding of love.

ANDREA SKEVINGTON

Where we give our attention

Jesus replied, 'A man was going down from Jerusalem to Jericho, and fell into the hands of robbers, who stripped him, beat him, and went away, leaving him half dead.'

What sort of things have, in the past, changed our views? Sometimes, compelling evidence will do so, but I also find my empathy is broadened by stories, whether from literature or life. Listening to people share their stories helps me see through their eyes.

Here, Jesus begins his story with this abrupt account of violence. Yet our concern is not with the robbers. Jesus gives them little attention – just this one verse, this list of cruelty. Imagine if we were telling this story. Imagine reading it in the newspapers. The robbers, and the details of the crime, would loom large. Jesus has a lesson for us in how we give our attention. Our attention is powerful; it shifts our internal landscape. It is naturally drawn to danger, threat and difficulty, and our internal territory can become a fearful road. Of course, we need to listen to our fears and take sensible actions, but runaway worry does not help us. In this crime story, Jesus gives due acknowledgement to the robbery and to the terrible harm it does, but that is not where he lingers.

The lack of detail about the wounded man has a different effect. There is nothing to identify him, and therefore we can all identify with him. It could be any one of the people listening; it could be us. How would we feel if it happened to us? Story opens our imagination and, through that, compassion and empathy. We can walk in this man's shoes. Our concern is with his suffering, and so we hope that someone might help him. As this man is Everyman, our circle of compassion is expanded. Whoever he is, we hope help comes.

As we wait with the wounded man, dare we open our hearts to him, despite the presence of fear and worry? Or perhaps we see ourselves coming along the road, wondering if we would have the courage to help? Or perhaps we are feeling helpless and waiting for those footsteps.

'I cry aloud to the Lord, and he answers me from his holy hill' (Psalm 3:4).

ANDREA SKEVINGTON

Religion can let you down

Now by chance a priest was going down that road; and when he saw him, he passed by on the other side. So likewise a Levite, when he came to the place and saw him, passed by on the other side.

These religious people also receive minimal attention. They appear briefly, passing by the injured man and through the story. I wonder if the lawyer's hopes rose at the mention of a priest and Levite. He may have expected them to be heroes of the story. Many of us will have felt let down at times by the actions of those who should have cared for us. Whether it is church leaders or others with responsibility, it can feel like betrayal. We may need to seek wise council and tend our wounds. It may take time and prayer.

On the other hand, we can represent God's people to those in need, and maybe we have let others down. It's uncomfortable to consider that we may not act with goodness or love, even if we are 'right'. If our interpretation of law or scripture does not lead to greater love of God and neighbour, perhaps we could think again.

There may have been reasons the priest and Levite walked by – reasons sanctioned by their faith. They may have been following purity laws, which forbade the touching of a body or blood. Maintaining personal purity may distance us and even harden our hearts. It can lead to walking by on the other side. As can fear.

Yet every day we see pain and suffering – too many people, too far away to be helped. What are we to do? I think our prayerful, humble, loving response may call us to help where we can, to be aware of our own limits and to not overlook those directly before us.

'You yourselves are our letter, written on our hearts, to be known and read by all; and you show that you are a letter of Christ, prepared by us, written not with ink but with the Spirit of the living God, not on tablets of stone but on tablets of human hearts' (2 Corinthians 3:2–3). May I allow my heart to be tender enough to live out the law of love today.

ANDREA SKEVINGTON

A practice to expand compassion

But a Samaritan while travelling came near him; and when he saw him, he was moved with pity. He went to him and bandaged his wounds, having poured oil and wine on them. Then he put him on his own animal, brought him to an inn, and took care of him. The next day he took out two denarii, gave them to the innkeeper, and said, 'Take care of him; and when I come back, I will repay you whatever more you spend.'

Now we reach the story's turn. At last, someone has come to help. But that someone is a Samaritan, a generational enemy, despised. Are we humble enough to look up to someone so unexpected?

We have asked what love looks like. We have asked how to cultivate love. Here Jesus sets out a process we can learn from. The Samaritan comes near, sees and is moved with pity. We can cultivate the practice of compassion by coming near, truly seeing and allowing ourselves to be moved. And, once moved, our heart overflows into action. Our daily lives bring us into contact with people. Dare we draw near?

As the robbers' actions were listed, so now the Samaritan's are – meeting the harms done point for point. Here is a model for dealing with pain, whether that of others or ourselves. For each wound, we show loving kindness.

Our capacity to be moved to pity, having hearts of flesh, is a sign of life and love in this story. It is also the spring from which loving action flows. It is a precious thing and can be cultivated. Important as giving money to charity is, there is something sacred and transforming about humbly serving and helping as this Samaritan did. I know my encounters with people living on the streets have changed me in ways that giving money alone cannot. We need to be wise and careful, but perhaps, rooted in the love of God, we can take a step.

Draw near. See. Be moved by pity. Go and do.

As we read these verses again, where do we see ourselves? The wounded man, the Samaritan, the innkeeper or someone watching? May God give us wisdom and courage as we seek to live from love.

ANDREA SKEVINGTON

Go and do

'Which of these three, do you think, was a neighbour to the man who fell into the hands of the robbers?' He said, 'The one who showed him mercy.' Jesus said to him, 'Go and do likewise.'

We return to the lawyer's question. It has a different weight now. It is no longer abstract, but a matter of life and death. Jesus subtly changes it. 'Who is my neighbour?' implies we can pick and choose. Jesus, by contrast, asks who *was* a neighbour to the wounded man. Neighbour is our identity, shown by what we do. Jesus might be implying that we are all neighbours to each other, and what matters is acting from that true nature. Perhaps, like the love of God, this love is not limited. Mercy is not a matter of law; it is an impulse we can cultivate. And mercy is not a matter for debate or analysis. It is demonstrated in heartfelt kindness.

And so the debate ends. For all so far has been words and talk. Now, Jesus tells the lawyer to go and do. Here is a deep and genuine challenge. The path of life looks like this – it looks like bending down to bandage someone's wounds; it looks like courage, mercy and humility; it looks like living out love. In order to even begin, I have found I need to be rooted in forms of prayer which cultivate love and acceptance of myself and others. I find daily prayers of blessing nurture loving kindness, as I gradually expand my circle of blessing. I find imaginative reading of scripture, too, cultivates compassion.

Like this: read the reflection below slowly, twice. The first time imagine you are the one lying wounded on the road speaking these words. The second time, think of the Samaritan, showing the face of God to the wounded one. Dare we ask for courage to go and do likewise? Could we be the goodness and mercy that attends someone's path?

Even though I walk through the darkest valley, I fear no evil; for you are with me… You prepare a table before me in the presence of my enemies; you anoint my head with oil; my cup overflows. Surely goodness and mercy shall follow me all the days of my life' (Psalm 23:4–6).

ANDREA SKEVINGTON

Who is welcome?

Now all the tax-collectors and sinners were coming near to listen to him. And the Pharisees and the scribes were grumbling and saying, 'This fellow welcomes sinners and eats with them.' So he told them this parable: 'Which one of you, having a hundred sheep and losing one of them, does not leave the ninety-nine in the wilderness and go after the one that is lost until he finds it? When he has found it, he lays it on his shoulders and rejoices.'

Jesus welcomed sinners – so the religious leaders complained. Jesus ate in all kinds of company, unconcerned for his reputation. His goodness took no pride in piety. He spent time with people most religious folk avoid. I have been seeking to change my own behaviour in the light of this. Increasingly, I see the Spirit working in a wider community, moving people to care for each other and creation. During the pandemic, our town has worked to share food in a kind of distributed kingdom feast.

Jesus challenges the religious leaders. Shepherds bring home lost sheep without condemning them. God values the lost, the rejected and the wanderers. Sometimes it seems that religious institutions do not. Jesus does not reject sinners; he welcomes them. He eats with them. God does not reject us but finds us and brings us home rejoicing. God trusts the righteous, leaves them and goes out of his way to seek the strays. You can't be a good shepherd without getting dirty, without risking thorns and wilderness, without long searching. Jesus led this hard life of a shepherd for our sakes.

So where are we in the story? It is easy to start as lost sheep, but gradually shift to be those who keep apart from others. So today, can we delight in the welcome Jesus gives? One way of doing this is to stop comparing ourselves to others, and simply rejoice that Jesus loves us, carries us home on his shoulders and welcomes us to his feast. Can we expand our vision to include people we might have overlooked? Can we, too, welcome as Jesus does?

'He tends his flock like a shepherd: he gathers the lambs in his arms and carries them close to his heart; he gently leads those that have young'
(Isaiah 40:11, NIV).

ANDREA SKEVINGTON

As precious as a silver coin

'Or what woman having ten silver coins, if she loses one of them, does not light a lamp, sweep the house, and search carefully until she finds it? When she has found it, she calls together her friends and neighbours, saying, "Rejoice with me, for I have found the coin that I had lost." Just so, I tell you, there is joy in the presence of the angels of God over one sinner who repents.'

The second short parable is also a question. Questions, as well as stories, open us to consider new things. Here we consider a woman searching for a lost coin. Jesus is gently expanding our vision. This is one of the few parables where a poor woman represents God. A poor woman hunting for one of her precious coins is an image of God's love for us.

As the crowd listened to this story, they will have felt her anxiety at her lost savings, her provision for hard times. But I wonder if they were also moved to think that, in this story, they are the treasure. They are so precious that God seeks them out.

The coin can do nothing to help itself be found. Sometimes, we feel like that. Sometimes, we can feel in such a dark place that we can't pray or seek help. Even so, we are God's treasure. He rejoices over us in love. In comparison to the vastness of God's love, our lostness is as small as a silver coin. Perhaps, in time, we can find this love and welcome is the route to our healing. Jesus, the light of the world, is a lamp held up to find us in the darkness.

The woman invites her friends and neighbours to celebrate. How precious it must have been for those listening to know that God celebrates them. Notice how this joy is shared, not solitary. Kingdom joy connects us to others, helps us expand our welcome. The question is, will the religious leaders take part in this joy?

As we read this parable again, see what strikes you. Perhaps you feel lost in a dark place or forgotten in a dusty corner. Imagine yourself as seen by God, as a bright coin worth searching for, worth rejoicing over.

ANDREA SKEVINGTON

What do we value about God?

Then Jesus said, 'There was a man who had two sons. The younger of them said to his father, "Father, give me the share of the property that will belong to me." So he divided his property between them. A few days later the younger son gathered all he had and travelled to a distant country, and there he squandered his property in dissolute living.'

We reach the remarkable climax of this series of stories. Its sharp focus is one aspect of the father – his abundant, almost reckless generosity and forgiveness. Jesus' listeners – including us – wonder: how might I respond? Which son might I be?

We begin with the younger. We imagine the father's pain at this bleak 'give me' – this cruel demand for advance payment. Talk of money recalls the lost coin, and we can reflect on what we treasure. In that parable, the coin represents a precious lost person. Here, the treasure – the inheritance – is a replacement for a relationship. It is so easy to only pray 'give me'. Can we know the love behind the generosity?

This parable shows the transactional relationships both sons have with their father. He, by contrast, is endlessly generous. They seem to be living in different worlds. The sons live in a world of lack and competition, while the father lives in a world of regenerative generosity. Perhaps we dare trust the never-ending love of the Father. I have found, in my faltering attempts at living generously and open-handedly, that there are many forms of riches and return: community, contentment, joy, connection.

The younger son sets out from this security. Staying put, spiritually, is not the way of growth. But walking away from what we have known can be painful as well as freeing. The younger son will face a hard road down.

Many of those drawn to Jesus are like this younger son. Maybe the love and acceptance Jesus showed them released them to grow and change. Maybe being with him is treasure enough. To be with him is to share in the abundant love of the Father. Can we be like a weaned child, not demanding, but held in loving arms?

'I have calmed and quieted my soul, like a weaned child with its mother'
(Psalm 131:2).

ANDREA SKEVINGTON

The discipline of dark places

When he had spent everything, a severe famine took place throughout that country, and he began to be in need. So he went and hired himself out to one of the citizens of that country, who sent him to his fields to feed the pigs. He would gladly have filled himself with the pods that the pigs were eating; and no one gave him anything.

We are far away from the father's house now, in the frightening world of scarcity and lack. Financial resources and harvests can fail, and an inheritance doesn't last forever. Jesus reports 'no one gave him anything'. It is the dark opposite of the generosity of the father. The gulf could not be greater.

The son has fallen far. It is terrifying to find ourselves, or to see a loved one, so desolate. Even here, it remains true that there is no place too dark, too low, for the loving heart of God to find us. We may know, or tell from our own experience, stories of people who have hit rock bottom and come to a place where their lives turned around. There are no guarantees, though. Some fall and do not rise again. So what helps us rise?

We think of young people as prodigals, but faith shifts and derailings also happen in later life. Can we become more accepting of inevitable change and difficulty? Can we seek the courage to find that treasure is hidden in these depths? Many spiritual writings talk of the dark night of the soul, the little way, the path of descent. Although the father's house is a place of plenty, absence and suffering are not signs of God's disfavour. It requires a deep surrender, a trust in the unseen faithfulness of whatever is holding us, even if we have lost sight of our old picture of God. Painfully, it is a place where growth can happen. That is not to say that suffering is God's plan or sent by God, but that the resurrection power is precisely that – it takes the worst and the darkest and brings forth something good. The seed falls to the ground and breaks open. Then, it grows.

'Blessed are you who are poor, for yours is the kingdom of God' (Luke 6:20).

ANDREA SKEVINGTON

Turning for home

'But when he came to himself he said, "How many of my father's hired hands have bread enough and to spare, but here I am dying of hunger! I will get up and go to my father, and I will say to him, 'Father, I have sinned against heaven and before you; I am no longer worthy to be called your son; treat me like one of your hired hands.'" So he set off and went to his father.'

There are moments on which whole lives turn. This is one such, when the younger son came to himself. He returned to his true self and saw things as they were. I love the idea of this repentance as coming to yourself, rather than self-rejection. We asked yesterday what helps. His previous experience of the love and generosity helped him come to himself. It is good to build families and communities where people experience acceptance.

Maybe yesterday, as we talked of rock bottom, you recalled a sharp moment of repentance. Maybe your life has seen less dramatic turnings around. I remember going to college with a hunger for meaning, for drawing closer to God. I noticed a loving community of Christians and took a step towards them. Dramatic or simple, we can have daily moments of awakening – coming to ourselves. Awareness gives us space where we can turn home.

The younger son's hunger sends him home. Pain can be a motivator for change, and such turnings are often painful. We can condemn ourselves. I find it helps to cultivate compassionate honesty rather than blame, even as we get up and set off for the Father's house. We can recognise we are children of a parent who loves and helps us. Knowing you have done wrong is a first step. But with that knowledge, we can hide and fake and blame others, or we can get up and walk towards the Father. This turn, and return, is what makes the difference.

We are not like the sheep and the coin. We have agency. We can turn around. We can receive the good that is offered us, or we can live as the son did, hungrily, as if he were unloved and fatherless.

Dare we believe that the Father wants us home?

ANDREA SKEVINGTON

The running father

'But while he was still far off, his father saw him and was filled with compassion; he ran and put his arms around him and kissed him… "Father, I have sinned…" But the father said to his slaves, "Quickly, bring out a robe – the best one – and put it on him; put a ring on his finger and sandals on his feet… and let us eat and celebrate; for this son of mine was dead and is alive again; he was lost and is found!"'

The father had not forgotten his son. He was keeping an eye on the road, on the distant horizon. The shepherd and the woman in the previous parables were active searchers. They went out of their way to seek. Not so here. We have such freedom to fail and fall, but love waits for us to turn towards home again.

Notice the father's response: a magnified version of the Samaritan's mercy. The Samaritan saw, felt pity and went. The loving father sees, is filled with compassion and runs and embraces. This moment reveals his heartbreak and joy. And, here too, actions meet needs point for point: finest food, finest clothes, community and love.

The father is not listening to his confession. He does not berate or shame the son, who faces no rebuke. He is home; that is enough. He is home, and he will be loved and feted. Those who have even momentarily lost a child will feel how tightly the father held him, how visceral the loss and joy.

As we imagine ourselves into this moment, do we know this welcome for ourselves? We need not fear rebuke. God is always watching the road, ready to welcome us home. Jesus tells us so in the parable and shows us by welcoming those listening to it.

So, they gather for a feast, and there is more than enough. We can ask for our daily bread as children. We do not have to earn it. The Father's table is wide and heaped with good things.

Take a moment to read the passage again, imagining yourself into the story. What might it mean for you today to live in the security of such love as this?

ANDREA SKEVINGTON

Righteous anger?

'Now his elder son was in the field; and when he came and approached the house, he heard music and dancing. He called one of the slaves and asked what was going on. He replied, "Your brother has come, and your father has killed the fatted calf, because he has got him back safe and sound." Then he became angry and refused to go in. His father came out and began to plead with him.'

Let's stay a moment with the younger son sitting in the place of honour, dressed in fine clothes. I think of him under his father's loving gaze, the finest garment of all. He is fed because he is hungry and home. Will this mercy open his eyes, shift his way of seeing, so he knows the depth of the father's love? Can we move from a 'cupboard love' for God to something deeper?

And now we turn to the older son, hard at work in the fields, returning home to hear music and dancing. We may have sympathy with the obedient older son. All his life he has worked for the father – 'slaved' is the word he uses. Suddenly, deeply buried motives and attitudes are revealed. It seems he is working for reward.

As the father comes out to him too, we see the depth of the difficulties reconciliation might pose. Real differences arise in families, communities and churches. We can do harm to each other, and anger is an important teacher, warning us of danger. Perhaps we can sit with these uncomfortable feelings and then sift them. We need caution where someone's behaviour has been damaging, but we can nevertheless let go of a desire for vengeance and bitterness.

This parable does not offer an easy answer, but a choice. Can the older son accept the father's mercy for another, or will he stay outside the feast? Both sons have misunderstood their father. Both have been distant from him. At this moment, one sits within the feast, perhaps with dawning awareness of how deeply he is loved. One is outside, hurt and angry. The feast is there, ready and waiting. Love would welcome them both.

'Even the sparrow finds a home… Happy are those who live in your house'
(Psalm 84:3–4).

ANDREA SKEVINGTON

The difficulties of acceptance

"'For all these years I have been working like a slave for you... yet you have never given me even a young goat... But when this son of yours came back... you killed the fatted calf...!" Then the father said to him, "Son, you are always with me, and all that is mine is yours. But we had to celebrate... because this brother of yours was dead and has come to life; he was lost and has been found.'"

The older son, previously so obedient, now reveals the depth of his resentment. He also reveals he has misunderstood his father profoundly. The older son feels entitled because of his service. Presumably, he believes that is what is required. It is not. He could have been living as the eldest son of a generous father, accepting everything the father has is his. He could have been working in response to the father's love as a gift, freely. For us, it is easy to begin a life of faith in this spirit, then come to think we are earning God's favour. We do not have to earn love. Neither do we have to look over our shoulder and see how God loves another.

Will the older son go in? The story does not tell us. He may not. To accept the father's invitation means to sit down next to his formerly disgraced brother. That is a hard thing to do. It means relinquishing any sense of superiority. It means accepting the father is free to invite whomever he wishes.

Jesus invites all to his feasts, older and younger sons both. And his listeners would have seen themselves as one or the other. The religious leaders would be aware that they were cast as the older, in this precarious, self-excluded condition. I wonder if they did sit down and eat with Jesus and his friends. Accepting that God loves and accepts people is a powerful step towards reconciliation and inclusion. It can help in those fractured relationships we have considered. It might help these brothers.

All are welcome to sit and feast together in the abundance of God's mercy: found, alive, home.

'In you my soul takes refuge; in the shadow of your wings I will take refuge' (Psalm 57:1).

ANDREA SKEVINGTON

Favourite prayers

Prayer is at the heart of the Christian experience and of the scriptures. From the first prayer in the Bible (Genesis 20:7 – a prayer for healing, in the context of Abraham's failure to trust God) to the repeated image in Revelation of the prayers of God's people rising as incense in heaven, we are shown the importance of prayer. We are told that God answers the prayers of his people; that Jesus spent much time in prayer; that down through the ages the people of God have been faithful and persistent in prayer; and that prayer has been at the heart of the great movements of God in the church and the wider world.

At one level prayer is simple, perhaps the only Christian activity that anyone, at any age or stage, can participate in, anytime, anywhere. Yet, if we're honest, for most of us prayer is a challenging topic. We find it difficult to define, uncomfortable to talk about and often nearly impossible to practise!

While the disciples aren't recorded asking Jesus to teach them to preach or perform miracles, they did ask to be taught to pray (Luke 11:1). And this in a culture where public prayer on street corners and in the marketplace as well as in the home would have been much more familiar than it is to most of us today. How many of us pray regularly as a family?

Almost inevitably, the very mystery of prayer means that it has been the subject of scientific enquiry: in one study, the effect of different types of prayers on brain activity was investigated. Praying nuns were literally put in a medical scanner, and it was found that various forms of prayer involved the engagement of differing areas of their brains. We won't be using any MRI scanners over the next few days, but we will look at some of the different types of prayers found in scripture. If you can, I would also encourage you to read and reflect on the words of James Montgomery's beautiful hymn 'Prayer is the soul's sincere desire':

Prayer is the Christian's vital breath,
The Christian's native air;
His watchword at the gates of death;
He enters rest with prayer.

MURDO MACDONALD

Anguished prayer

In her deep anguish Hannah prayed to the Lord, weeping bitterly… As she kept on praying to the Lord, Eli observed her mouth. Hannah was praying in her heart, and her lips were moving but her voice was not heard. Eli thought she was drunk and said to her, 'How long are you going to stay drunk? Put away your wine'… Hannah replied, 'I am a woman who is deeply troubled. I have not been drinking wine or beer; I was pouring out my soul to the Lord… I have been praying here out of my great anguish and grief.' Eli answered, 'Go in peace, and may the God of Israel grant you what you have asked of him.'

While many of us will have called out in prayer from the depths of despair, few of us will have gone through the experience that Hannah faced. Taunted for years by a rival wife over her failure to produce a son, Hannah found herself using the annual family trip to offer the sacrifice at Shiloh to pour out her heart in desperation to God. As if this wasn't humiliation enough, she then found herself being accused by the priest of effectively being drunk and disorderly in church.

Can you imagine how Hannah felt? It would have been easy for her not only to be angry with Eli, with her circumstances and with God, but also to give up hope. And yet, despite her grief and anguish, she persevered in prayer and, as we know, she was eventually vindicated. More than that, she remained true to her promise to dedicate her son Samuel to God's service.

Jesus encourages us, his followers, to persevere in prayer – see, for example, his parable of the persistent widow (Luke 18:1–5). While many of us may give up too easily on praying for a situation, we also recognise that one of the many challenges we face in praying is to know when to keep asking and when to accept that the request that we are bringing to God isn't in line with his perfect will.

'Father, give us courage to change what must be altered, serenity to accept what cannot be helped, and the insight to know the one from the other'
(attributed to Reinhold Niebuhr, 1892–1971).

MURDO MACDONALD

Prayer of frustration

But when they said, 'Give us a king to lead us,' this displeased Samuel; so he prayed to the Lord. And the Lord told him: 'Listen to all that the people are saying to you; it is not you they have rejected, but they have rejected me as their king. As they have done from the day I brought them up out of Egypt until this day, forsaking me and serving other gods, so they are doing to you. Now listen to them; but warn them solemnly and let them know what the king who will reign over them will claim as his rights.'

Sometimes we face situations which frustrate or annoy us: circumstances don't work out as hoped, people let us down or, as in this Bible passage, others make what we know to be the wrong decision.

The question is: how do we react in such situations? The answer, as we know in theory, is that we should take the situation to God in prayer. However, we also know that, for most of us, the practice isn't always as easy as the theory. We perhaps try to resolve the situation using our own abilities (bang some metaphorical heads together) or maybe we wash our hands of it, hoping all turns out right in the end.

Samuel realised his fellow Israelites' decision to follow the ways of the world around them – to appoint a king to rule over them (v. 5) – was the wrong one. He took it as a personal slight, but his reaction wasn't to take the huff, bury his head in the sand or confront those making the mistake, all actions which most of us would be tempted to do when faced with similar circumstances. Instead, in his anger Samuel took the right course: he prayed about it. The somewhat surprising answer he received from God was to allow the people to follow this wrong path, but also to issue a stern warning of the consequences.

When we pray, there will be times when we will receive similarly surprising responses from God. Our responsibility is, like Samuel, to remain faithful.

'O what peace we often forfeit,
O what needless pain we bear,
all because we do not carry
everything to God in prayer'
(Joseph Scriven, 1819–86).

MURDO MACDONALD

Name it and claim it?

Jabez was more honourable than his brothers. His mother had named him Jabez, saying, 'I gave birth to him in pain.' Jabez cried out to the God of Israel, 'Oh, that you would bless me and enlarge my territory! Let your hand be with me, and keep me from harm so that I will be free from pain.' And God granted his request.

Favourite prayers? Yes, there are undoubtedly prayers in the Bible which bring great comfort, but, if we're honest, especially in the Old Testament, there are also examples which leave us squirming. Some of what the psalmists pray for in terms of retribution (see, for example, Psalms 69 and 109) doesn't sit easily with Christ's instruction to love our enemies and to do good to those who oppose us.

Today's scripture includes a prayer which in many ways makes me feel uncomfortable: it seems, at first sight, to be all about me, me, me. Maybe that's why I'm so discomfited: much as I would like to think of myself as more spiritual, is this in effect a mirror, reminding me that too many of my prayers have my own interests front and centre?

It also seems to be very close to what has become known as a 'prosperity gospel', where what is being requested ('enlarge my territory!') is physical, worldly riches, rather than the more spiritual aims which we feel should be our focus.

Yet there is much we can learn from Jabez: despite having had a difficult start in life (his name means 'sorrowful'), he is described as honourable. In a culture where there were many gods who could be worshipped, his focus was on the one true God. Who of us hasn't, like Jabez, sought God's protection and guidance?

And the glorious truth which runs like a thread through all of scripture is that, despite our insignificance and obscurity, God *does* care for us, his people – for all the small details, as well as the big decisions.

Pray for people known to you who may face pain, rejection, want or loss. Give thanks that God is able to fulfil all our needs.

MURDO MACDONALD

Praying for strength

Then, the fifth time, Sanballat sent his assistant to me with the same message… I sent him this reply: 'Nothing like what you are saying is happening; you are just making it up out of your head.' They were all trying to frighten us, thinking, 'Their hands will get too weak for the work, and it will not be completed.' But I prayed, 'Now strengthen my hands.'

Have you ever cried out, as Nehemiah does here, 'God, give me strength'? His cry is partly born of frustration with the persistent opposition he faces. We are told that this is the fifth occasion on which his enemies have tried to deflect Nehemiah from the work of rebuilding the city walls. His response to this opposition has consistently been faithfulness in both work and prayer.

When I was asked to write this series, one of my initial thoughts was the famous 'arrow' prayer found in Nehemiah 2:4, one of my favourite examples in all of scripture of a quick prayer offered in a time of crisis. In that situation, Nehemiah was put on the spot by King Artaxerxes, whom he was serving: an immediate response was required. This incident, however, is different; Nehemiah has time to formulate his answer.

Prayer is a theme which runs through the book of Nehemiah. The narrative repeatedly makes clear that his actions and decisions are guided by God, that he brings all before the Lord. But Nehemiah is a man of action. He doesn't just pray for discernment; he also leads people forward in the strength which God supplies, a prime example of the need to sometimes be the answer to our own prayers.

Not only can we empathise with Nehemiah in his frustration and his facing down threats, we can also learn from him. In our own experience, there are occasions when we have time to consider our course of action, but there are other situations when a speedy decision and decisive response is what is required.

*'Soldiers of Christ, arise, and put your armour on,
strong in the strength which God supplies, through his eternal Son;
strong in the Lord of Hosts, and in his mighty pow'r,
who in the strength of Jesus trusts is more than conqueror'*
(Charles Wesley, 1707–88).

MURDO MACDONALD

Wrestling in prayer

'Now my soul is troubled, and what shall I say? "Father, save me from this hour"? No, it was for this very reason I came to this hour. Father, glorify your name!' Then a voice came from heaven, 'I have glorified it, and will glorify it again.'

It is clear from the gospel narratives that prayer was at the heart of all that Jesus did. We read of him seeking private places for prayer, and he often reminds his disciples that much prayer is needed for the tasks which faced them.

Jesus' communication took many forms – instruction, admonition, encouragement. A master storyteller, his parables still resonate with meaning down through the centuries. However, I was surprised to learn that, although many of Jesus' words are recorded for us in the gospels, we have relatively few examples of his praying. In fact, only seven of his prayers have been documented. Some examples are familiar to us, such as what we know as the Lord's Prayer (Matthew 6:9–13) and his prayer in John 17 just before his crucifixion.

The passage here contains both a hypothetical and an actual prayer of Jesus and brings into focus one of the central dilemmas we often find ourselves in when we pray. Faced with a tough situation, should our request be that God remove the difficulty? Jesus is clearly troubled: should he ask God to take him out of the situation or to bring him through it?

We need to be reminded repeatedly that our ultimate aim should be to bring glory to God: as the writers of the Westminster Shorter Catechism put it, 'Man's chief end is to glorify God.' There will be occasions when God will rescue us from a situation, but there will also be times when we need to face up to the trial, in order that God might be glorified in us.

'"My grace is sufficient for you, for my power is made perfect in weakness." Therefore I will boast all the more gladly about my weaknesses, so that Christ's power may rest on me. That is why, for Christ's sake, I delight in weaknesses, in insults, in hardships, in persecutions, in difficulties. For when I am weak, then I am strong' (2 Corinthians 12:9–10).

MURDO MACDONALD

Praying for others

For this reason I kneel before the Father, from whom every family in heaven and on earth derives its name. I pray that out of his glorious riches he may strengthen you with power through his Spirit in your inner being, so that Christ may dwell in your hearts through faith. And I pray that you, being rooted and established in love, may have power, together with all the Lord's holy people, to grasp how wide and long and high and deep is the love of Christ, and to know this love that surpasses knowledge – that you may be filled to the measure of all the fullness of God.

One of the joys of being a scientist is the opportunity to explore the majesty of the world around us, and indeed beyond. My own area of expertise, molecular biology, deals with the sub-microscopic world of the cell and its inner workings, while others explore the vastness of the universe which we glimpse as we look up to a starry sky.

While science allows us to measure many things, and this can often be very enlightening, we also realise that there are aspects of our experience which are simply impossible to quantify. How do we measure care or compassion, for example?

We all know that we should pray for others, but often find it difficult to know exactly what to pray for them. While we know our own needs, and these requests find their way to the top of our prayer lists, we sometimes struggle to know what it is we should pray when we bring others before God.

When it comes to praying for others, the apostle Paul is an excellent model. In his letters, he frequently refers to his persistent and impassioned prayer for the believers to whom he is writing. In this passage, his prayer is that we, as followers of Christ, would catch a fresh vision of the unknowable, boundless love and grace of God – and, as a result, we would be renewed in our worship of the God of all glory.

'For the love of God is broader than the measure of our mind; and the heart of the eternal is most wonderfully kind' (Frederick William Faber, 1814–63).

MURDO MACDONALD

Prayer and practice

Is anyone among you in trouble? Let them pray. Is anyone happy? Let them sing songs of praise. Is anyone among you ill? Let them call the elders of the church to pray over them and anoint them with oil in the name of the Lord. And the prayer offered in faith will make the sick person well; the Lord will raise them up. If they have sinned, they will be forgiven. Therefore confess your sins to each other and pray for each other so that you may be healed. The prayer of a righteous person is powerful and effective.

How often do we find ourselves saying something like, 'Well, there's not much we can do other than pray,' as though praying about a situation or issue is a last resort, when all other, more 'practical', options are exhausted? This is surely an upside-down view of what prayer is about. It should be fundamental to all that we do, the first thing that we turn to rather than the last. I recall a preacher saying, 'We don't pray *for* the work of God; prayer *is* the work of God.'

The letter of James is intensely practical. Indeed, it has sometimes been criticised for being too practical. However, as this passage makes clear, while living out our faith is important, prayer must be the basis of all that we seek to do in serving God.

Prayer for miraculous healing, linked to a ceremony as described in this passage, isn't something which is part of the evangelical Presbyterian tradition to which I belong. In all my years as an elder, I have never been called upon to anoint any of my parishioners with oil! While some would argue that the modern equivalent would be the prescription and administration of medical treatment, there are surely times when we fail to fully appreciate the difference that prayer and spiritual engagement with a situation or challenge could make. As a result, we may muddle through, but we miss out on a potentially far greater blessing.

If only we had prayed.

Let's be prayerful and practical: lift up before God people you know who are in trouble, who are happy or who are sick. And be assured that God hears and answers our prayers.

MURDO MACDONALD

1 and 2 Chronicles:
all time is in God's hands

 Are you someone who holds on to the past and doesn't like change? Do you like to think that things were better before? Alternatively, are you are someone who thinks that we should let go of the past and move on? Then 1 and 2 Chronicles could be the books for you, because the theme of Chronicles is the nature of God's guidance over time.

The message of the two books is that when you are able to draw strength and take comfort from God's faithfulness to you in the past, you can look confidently towards the future – 'Learn from the past; live in the present; prepare for the future.'

The very fact of the existence of 1 and 2 Chronicles is a tribute to the faith of Ezra, who is traditionally identified as its author. The book of Ezra is seen as a continuation of the text of 2 Chronicles. Originally a single book, 1 and 2 Chronicles was written in the middle of the Israelites' time in exile in preparation for their return. It was written in the fourth century BC, though not published until the third century BC. It was written ready for the descendants of the Israelites, who would be restored to their homeland in Judah after the exile. It was written to teach those alive after the exile of their history and their heritage as the people of God.

The Israelites were going back to what they saw as the land of promise but what in reality was a Jerusalem that had been destroyed (Nehemiah 2:11–20). The chronicler's message is one of hope, of expectation for the future. God has been faithful in the past and will be so again in the future: 'Forget the former things; do not dwell on the past. See, I am doing a new thing!' (Isaiah 43:18–19, NIV).

The Chronicles narrative begins with Adam and is carried forward, almost entirely through genealogical lists, to the restoration of the temple in Jerusalem and the return of the exiles. There are 200 names in the first chapter alone of people who have carried the word of God through the generations; the countless people who are the army of the living God.

BOB MAYO

God works through all ages

Adam, Seth, Enosh, Kenan, Mahalalel, Jared, Enoch, Methuselah, Lamech, Noah. The sons of Noah: Shem, Ham and Japheth… The sons of Abraham: Isaac and Ishmael…. David reigned in Jerusalem thirty-three years… All Israel was listed in the genealogies recorded in the book of the kings of Israel and Judah. They were taken captive to Babylon because of their unfaithfulness.

The books of 1 and 2 Chronicles trace the time of Israel going from the exile back to Adam. The genealogy would have had a powerful relevance for the returning exiles. Despite returning to a city in ruins (Nehemiah 1:3), they would be able to see that they were a part of God's people and of his plans for the future.

The books of Chronicles are also the final two books of the Hebrew Bible. They set up a platform for the New Testament. They begin with a genealogy and end with the great commission for the king to rebuild the temple. Matthew's gospel then also begins with a genealogy and ends with the great commission – not for building the temple, but the church.

Chronicles provides the architecture to God's plan of salvation that leads from the first to the second Adam. The genealogy links the history of Israel, from Adam onwards, with the coming of Christ. Matthew's genealogy traces Jesus back to Abraham. The Chronicles genealogy traces Abraham back to Adam (1 Chronicles 1:1–27). Thus, we see that 1 and 2 Chronicles links with Matthew and connects Adam with Christ. Matthew shows us that Jesus is descended from the house of David. Chronicles shows that the house of David is of the lineage of Adam and reaches out to the entire human race.

God's work of restoration down through history points to the arrival of the last Adam, the Son of God – 'So it is written: "The first man Adam became a living being"; the last Adam, a life-giving spirit' (1 Corinthians 15:45). This Son will be the true king.

Help me to rejoice that Jesus is the Lord of history and that he has all our times in his hands. Just as Israel waited for Christ's first coming, give me the faith to wait for his second coming.

BOB MAYO

God works through all people

David reigned in Jerusalem thirty-three years, and these were the children born to him there: Shammua, Shobab, Nathan and Solomon. These four were by Bathsheba daughter of Ammiel. There were also Ibhar, Elishua, Eliphelet, Nogah, Nepheg, Japhia, Elishama, Eliada and Eliphelet – nine in all. All these were the sons of David, besides his sons by his concubines. And Tamar was their sister.

The inclusion of Tamar in a long list of male names is startling. Tamar was raped by her half-brother Amnon (2 Samuel 13). Scripture then says that 'Amnon hated her with intense hatred. In fact, he hated her more than he had loved her… "Get this woman out of my sight and bolt the door after her"' (2 Samuel 13:15, 17). Tamar must have been an impressive figure. Who knows what respect she must have commanded in the community to be included in Chronicles as a significant figure in the history of Israel; to be listed as a part of the lineage of David to Adam; to have her name remembered here for eternity? Bad things happen to good people, but good can come from evil, even when we cannot see God's plan or understand it.

Tamar would probably never have known the significance her life would come to hold. She can be taken to represent the people whose story we do not know, who may have some unspeakable tragedy of which we are not aware. She is an inspiration to those of us who have had to overcome difficult circumstances in our own life.

Matthew lists four female ancestors of Jesus, none of whom had orthodox lives: Tamar (a different one), who seduced her father-in-law Judah so that she could conceive; Rahab the prostitute, who helped Joshua capture the city of Jericho; loyal Ruth, who was not even Jewish but a Moabite, and thus a foreigner from an enemy nation; and Bathsheba, who was the mother of King Solomon and the most powerful woman of her generation.

Thank you for brave lives lived by women who may have faced unspeakable tragedy, often without the credit they deserve.

BOB MAYO

God is in the ordinary events
of everyday life

But will God really dwell on earth with humans? The heavens, even the highest heavens, cannot contain you. How much less this temple I have built! Yet, Lord my God, give attention to your servant's prayer and his plea for mercy. Hear the cry and the prayer that your servant is praying in your presence. May your eyes be open towards this temple day and night, this place of which you said you would put your Name there. May you hear the prayer your servant prays towards this place. Hear the supplications of your servant and of your people Israel when they pray towards this place. Hear from heaven, your dwelling-place; and when you hear, forgive.

The title of 1 and 2 Chronicles in the Hebrew Bible is 'the events of the days'. In the Septuagint (the Greek translation of the Hebrew) the title is 'things left out'. The reason for this apparent paradox is that Chronicles tells the stories of God's work in a nation's life. God's work in our lives is at one and the same time 'the events of the days' and 'things [that can easily be] left out'.

With the building of the temple, the ability of the Israelites to understand God's will is seen as being determined less by prophetic speakers or ecstatic utterances than by the written word and faithful living. The temple marked the changeover from the prophets to the proverbs. Solomon rebuilt the temple so that the ark of the covenant could be housed and the Israelites could worship the Lord. He began to write the book of Proverbs so that his people might live out God's teaching in their day-to-day living.

In Chronicles the divine presence is always presumed in the ordinary events of life. Those who seek God's way and choose to do his will experience blessings; those who turn away from God experience judgement. Chronicles occupies a critical moment in Israelite history, as it begins the shift from mythic revelations and interventions to the written word as an indication of God's will.

Dear God, help me to see you in the ordinary events of everyday life.

BOB MAYO

New beginnings

All these were fighting men who volunteered to serve in the ranks. They came to Hebron fully determined to make David king over all Israel. All the rest of the Israelites were also of one mind to make David king. The men spent three days there with David, eating and drinking, for their families had supplied provisions for them. Also, their neighbours from as far away as Issachar, Zebulun and Naphtali came bringing food on donkeys, camels, mules and oxen. There were plentiful supplies of flour, fig cakes, raisin cakes, wine, olive oil, cattle and sheep, for there was joy in Israel.

In this passage we see the desire of the Israelites to make David their king. David's past misdemeanours are put behind him as he gets ready for his new role, for which God has been preparing him, as king of Israel. There are three days of feasting and celebration as David prepares for a new future.

Chronicles establishes how people are not locked into destructive patterns of sin, automatically repeated across different generations. The chronicler shows us the repentance of David and Hezekiah, and even the worst king of all, Manasseh, turns to God and is forgiven and patterns of life are changed (2 Chronicles 33:10–20). And the biggest reverse of all is that even the tragedy of the exile to Babylon is not the end of God's plans for his people. God forgives his people and brings them back to the land.

Chronicles shows how God is bigger than our past. God's grace (and forgiveness) is more powerful than any sin we may have committed, mistake we might have made or accident we may have caused. A life of faith means constant new beginnings. There is also nothing in our own story able to block the work of God's grace. Chronicles offers us a constant reminder of the unending movement of God's grace and forgiveness through the generations.

Dear Lord, thank you that you are bigger than all of our mistakes.
Even if we give up on you, thank you that we can be sure that
you will never give up on us.

BOB MAYO

Praise God's holy name

David praised the Lord in the presence of the whole assembly, saying, 'Praise be to you, Lord, the God of our father Israel, from everlasting to everlasting. Yours, Lord, is the greatness and the power and the glory and the majesty and the splendour, for everything in heaven and earth is yours. Yours, Lord, is the kingdom; you are exalted as head over all. Wealth and honour come from you; you are the ruler of all things. In your hands are strength and power to exalt and give strength to all. Now, our God, we give you thanks, and praise your glorious name. But who am I, and who are my people, that we should be able to give as generously as this? Everything comes from you, and we have given you only what comes from your hand.'

This passage contains within it the soundtrack to Israel's history: worship is at the centre of everything. It is not military skill or political expertise that makes Israel who it is; rather, it is the worship of the living God that brings Israel together as one people. This passage reminds us that a busy church programme of events, a full church or a concern for social justice are nothing if they don't flow from a community centred around worshipping and enjoying God.

David's words of praise, used in the Anglican Eucharistic prayer, contain within them the heart of true worship: we offer back to God only what he has already given to us. All of us are asked to freely and joyfully choose God, but we cannot do this unless God first works a new life in our hearts. What Chronicles calls us to is a participation in God's ongoing work of grace, a free giving of ourselves which flows from a recognition that faith does not depend on us and our own strength but upon God's Holy Spirit and what he has already done for us through Christ.

'And whatever you do, whether in word or deed, do it all in the name of the Lord Jesus, giving thanks to God the Father through him' (Colossians 3:17). Help us to worship you, God, in all things.

BOB MAYO

Solomon asks for wisdom

David said, 'My son Solomon is young and inexperienced, and the house to be built for the Lord should be of great magnificence and fame and splendour in the sight of all the nations. Therefore I will make preparations for it.' So David made extensive preparations before his death… That night God appeared to Solomon and said to him, 'Ask for whatever you want me to give you.' Solomon answered God, 'You have shown great kindness to David my father and have made me king in his place. Now, Lord God, let your promise to my father David be confirmed, for you have made me king over a people who are as numerous as the dust of the earth. Give me wisdom and knowledge, that I may lead this people, for who is able to govern this great people of yours?'

Building the temple in Jerusalem would have been the crowning moment of David's life. He had come from being a shepherd boy to being king of Israel. He had danced with joy as the ark of the covenant had come into Jerusalem and had taken a personal interest in measuring out the space where the temple would be built.

However, he was not the one that would build the temple. David is old, and the responsibility would fall to his son Solomon. Just as Moses did not enter into the promised land (Deuteronomy 32:51–52), it is not always the one that does the hard work that reaps the reward: 'Thus the saying "One sows and another reaps" is true' (John 4:37). The apostle Paul writes: 'I planted the seed, Apollos watered it, but God has been making it grow. So neither the one who plants nor the one who waters is anything, but only God, who makes things grow' (1 Corinthians 3:6–7).

At the start of his reign Solomon showed himself to be the right person for the challenge of building the temple and asked for wisdom from God for the task set before him. There are no limits to what can be achieved as long as we don't mind who gets the credit.

Lord, let me not mind if someone else gets the credit,
as long as you get the glory.

BOB MAYO

God over all the world

The Lord moved the heart of Cyrus king of Persia to make a proclamation throughout his realm and also to put it in writing: 'This is what Cyrus king of Persia says: "The Lord, the God of heaven, has given me all the kingdoms of the earth and he has appointed me to build a temple for him at Jerusalem in Judah. Any of his people among you may go up, and may the Lord their God be with them."'

Cyrus conquered Babylon in 539BC and was the most powerful man of his time. The fact that God used him to build the temple in Jerusalem shows the wideness of God's grace. It shows how God can use anyone, believer or not, to fulfil his divine purpose. According to Isaiah, God anointed Cyrus for this task (rebuilding the temple), even referring to him as a 'messiah' (anointed one): 'This is what the Lord says to his anointed, to Cyrus' (Isaiah 45:1). Cyrus is the only non-Jewish figure in the Bible to be called so.

It is easy for us to get into the trap of believing that God will use us more if we are more committed to him. The truth is that God uses the most unlikely people to fulfil his purpose. In the parable of the workers in the vineyard, everyone is treated the same however long or short a time they have worked during the day: 'the last will be first, and the first will be last' (Matthew 20:16).

The story of Cyrus shows God's purpose being fulfilled through the government of the day, and we are asked to pray for those in authority (1 Timothy 2:2). Surprising people from unexpected places will be the agents of God's redemption. The Spirit of God is too powerful to be restricted to church services and to be left exclusively to believers. In God, everything is through grace, and we will often be taken by surprise at what God has done. 'The wind blows wherever it pleases. You hear its sound, but you cannot tell where it comes from or where it is going. So it is with everyone born of the Spirit' (John 3:8).

God, keep me generous and open-hearted when you draw on unexpected people to further your kingdom in unexpected ways.

BOB MAYO

Sharing resources

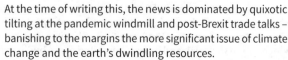

At the time of writing this, the news is dominated by quixotic tilting at the pandemic windmill and post-Brexit trade talks – banishing to the margins the more significant issue of climate change and the earth's dwindling resources.

Around 1970 we reached the point where our consumption couldn't be replenished. In 2021, Earth Overshoot Day – when consumption outstrips the planet's eco-resources which can be produced in twelve months – arrived on 29 July. So the question of resources – those things which we can use to make our lives better – is more urgent now than when Luke wrote about the early church in Acts 2. Undoubtedly, we will live within the means of nature; the only question is whether we do it by disaster or by design.

This disturbing global perspective underlines the need for wisdom, restraint and a commitment to pray for those who may need to take unpopular decisions. It can be quite a challenge to keep this perspective at the forefront of our minds when, for most of us, our immediate needs are being easily met and the only reminders we get are the appeal flyers in our newspapers. Given that global communication means that none of us can plead ignorance as a defence, it becomes our responsibility. And the big issues can leave us feeling desperately inadequate.

On a more general, local and personal level, though, Mother Teresa reminds us that if we have no peace, it is because we have forgotten that we belong to each other. Writing as one with a sad tendency to stubborn independence, I nevertheless have to acknowledge that I am unconsciously depending on others all the time, for food, water, electricity, medicine and a million other things. And, of course, we are not just talking material things: sharing ourselves, rejoicing with those who rejoice, weeping with those who weep, listening and laughing are perhaps even more vital at times.

Our reflections will aim to range widely, not forgetting, as Billy Graham reminds us, that it's a two-way process: 'God has given us two hands – one to receive with and the other to give with. We are not cisterns made for hoarding, we are channels made for sharing.'

SHEILA WALKER

I need you

Then the Lord God said, 'It is not good that the man should be alone; I will make him a helper as his partner'... Then the man said, 'This at last is bone of my bones and flesh of my flesh; this one shall be called Woman, for out of Man this one was taken.' Therefore a man leaves his father and his mother and clings to his wife, and they become one flesh.

In these verses, we see that right from the beginning it was never God's intention that we should be independent. Adam may have been the pinnacle of God's creation to date, but he was not complete. It was not that he didn't have plenty to occupy him; having dominion over the rest of the created world was arguably varied, challenging and satisfying work. It wasn't that he lacked abundant provision in material terms. But still there was a void – not only was he alone, but lonely. Other kinds of creatures could not fill that void; he could become complete only in partnership with one of the same kind as himself.

Those who live alone may often enjoy the company of a pet, be it cat or canary, and certainly animals can fulfil a real need. But it is not the same as a relationship with a human friend or family member, and we see here that God does not intend us to settle for second best. Some of us may live alone either by choice or because of circumstance, but that should not prevent us from fulfilling God's intention for us to take part in community in some way. This is how we will best realise our God-given potential.

The implications of these verses surely take us wider than marriage. 'Partnership' implies a sharing of all we are thinking, planning and doing: a joint effort to make the most of life. And this is true of any human relationship, be it between friends, family, neighbours or even with those we've never met but know of through the media.

Creator God, thank you for making us interdependent;
help us to recognise our need of one another and to respond accordingly.

SHEILA WALKER

Just the leftovers?

When [Ruth] got up to glean, Boaz instructed his young men, 'Let her glean even among the standing sheaves, and do not reproach her. You must also pull out some handfuls for her from the bundles, and leave them for her to glean, and do not rebuke her.' So she gleaned in the field until evening. then she beat out what she had gleaned, and it was about an ephah of barley.

The story of Ruth provides a beautiful illustration of the God-given instruction in Leviticus about gleaning: that landowners are not to reap to the very edge of their fields or gather every last grape from the vine, but should leave some pickings for the poor and needy. When this command is repeated in Deuteronomy, there is the added promise of blessing for such landowners.

Perhaps we might be tempted to protest, on two counts: that there is an acceptance of the fact that there will always be those who are poor and needy, and that this appears a somewhat parsimonious and erratic provision for them.

In response to the first objection, we surely have only to look around or, if we are privileged to live in a wealthy area, to look at information from any major aid agency to know that poverty appears inevitable, even in countries which are sufficiently wealthy to support all their citizens. Such is the mix of greed, indifference, incompetence and the corruption of power that form part of our human nature. It is true that agencies are making inroads in many places through community transformation and self-sustainability programmes, but utopia is surely beyond us: that is, until Christ returns and the kingdom of heaven comes in fullness.

For this reason, both Old and New Testaments are full of repeated injunctions to care for the poor, often the orphans, widows and strangers in our midst. But only to share the leftovers after the rich have taken their fill? Maybe there is a positive here: that those who have limited resources are given the dignity of becoming partners, co-workers, rather than simply being dependent on hand-outs. Sharing is not only about material things.

Lord, help us to support those agencies which combine generosity with building sustainable communities and restoring personal dignity. Amen

SHEILA WALKER

Word in action

When you stretch out your hands, I will hide my eyes from you; even though you make many prayers, I will not listen; your hands are full of blood. Wash yourselves, make yourselves clean; remove the evil of your doings from before my eyes; cease to do evil, learn to do good; seek justice, rescue the oppressed, defend the orphan, plead for the widow.

Isaiah refers to the recipients at the beginning of this prophecy as Sodom and Gomorrah – a painful allusion to the fact that Israel's behaviour is just as displeasing to God as that of these two notorious cities. Israel at the end of King Uzziah's reign had seen the rich getting richer as the poor became poorer. Sound all too familiar? Hence Isaiah's stern rebuke to the worshipping community that no amount of ritual or even prayer counts for anything with God unless it is accompanied by an outworking of faith in terms of an active concern for justice and mercy.

This is, of course, a perennial challenge. James, in his epistle, writes forcefully about faith without works being dead, and there are surely times for all of us when this resonates all too clearly in our own lives. The gift so many of us enjoy in our rich, Bible-based services and liturgies will often see us needing to use those words as prayers rather than proclamation. Yes, we do believe, but we need the Lord to deal with the unbelief that can make us stop short of translating that faith into action, especially when its outworking may call on us to make sacrifices.

If Christ's disciples are to be known by their love for one another rather than as hypocrites, words and actions must match. This must prompt us not only to respond as individuals and to challenge systemic injustice, but also to check that our worship is humble and honest, recognising our shortcomings and asking the Lord to enable us to hear the pleas of those needy individuals behind the generalities of our prayers. In sharing our riches with them, we share with him.

Lord Jesus, may we be people of integrity, whose words, worship and actions match and who are known for our sincerity and sacrificial sharing.

SHEILA WALKER

Trustees for God

Is not this the fast that I choose… Is it not to share your bread with the hungry, and bring the homeless poor into your house; when you see the naked, to cover them, and not to hide yourself from your own kin? Then your light shall break forth like the dawn, and your healing shall spring up quickly; your vindicator shall go before you, the glory of the Lord shall be your rearguard.

In the previous verses, the Lord challenges the hollowness of the people's fasting. The law of Moses prescribed fasting only on the Day of Atonement, but fasts also came to be proclaimed in times of national emergency and, following the destruction of Jerusalem, became regular events. All good, but with the danger of degenerating into mere ritual, where self-righteous piety replaces true repentance and integrity of word and action.

True fasting leaves us with few escape routes or excuses. We cannot rest content while hunger, homelessness and poverty remain. Charity may begin among our own kin; it is not to end there. We find here a key principle: when our fast is from 'ownership', God is able to pour out his blessing on us. It is when we seek to save our lives that, in the truest sense, we lose them; when we trust God enough to abandon everything to him, knowing it is his anyway, he is able to fill our empty hands with all we need.

Hudson Taylor, missionary to China, tells of the time he had only a half-crown left to his name and came upon a beggar. 'If only I had shillings and a sixpence, I would surely give him something,' he thought. But somehow he felt unable to pass by and, after a severe wrestling with his Lord, gave the half-crown to the beggar. Returning home, he felt at peace but vulnerable; the following day, he received an anonymous gift of a half-sovereign.

This is not to say that we are deliberately to put God to the test, or that such immediate cause and effect is guaranteed; rather, the point is that our trust is in an utterly faithful and loving God.

Lord, give us grace to trust you enough to come to you
with empty hands. Amen

SHEILA WALKER

Fair trade

Hear this, you that trample on the needy, and bring to ruin the poor of the land, saying 'When will the new moon be over so that we may sell grain; and the sabbath, so that we may offer wheat for sale? We will make the ephah small and the shekel great, and practise deceit with false balances, buying the poor for silver and the needy for a pair of sandals, and selling the sweepings of the wheat.' The Lord has sworn by the pride of Jacob: Surely I will never forget any of their deeds.

Amos, a shepherd from the south, is sent to prophesy to the northern kingdom of Israel, and a key part of his message is to warn of God's impending judgement. They have paid only lip service to God, neglected the poor and sought their own well-being at the expense of others; they will therefore be taken into exile.

Sin can be both individual and systemic, and it's easy to take refuge in the latter. 'Everyone is doing it,' we say. 'It's just the way things are. We have to play the game if we're to earn a living, and what's wrong with being successful in business? We can even give some to charity.'

Does the end justify the means? Rarely. God calls us to be faithful in small things in order that we may be trusted with more. Worldly success may call not for praise but for judgement, depending on how it is acquired. In the case of the merchants in Israel, fair dealings in the first place would have lessened the need for any 'charitable giving' with its inherent danger of self-righteousness.

Systemic injustice can be stubborn, but that is no reason not to campaign and use whatever influence we have, such as to refuse to support the big names who do not pay their small suppliers on time, or to lobby for fair distribution of medical supplies to those who most need them.

It's all too easy to choose to forget that God is a God of justice as well as mercy, and is well aware of all those little compromises we'd rather gloss over.

Lord, purify our hearts, that all our dealings with others
may err on the side of generosity. Amen

SHEILA WALKER

It's all yours

We want you to know, brothers and sisters, about the grace of God that has been granted to the churches of Macedonia; for during a severe ordeal of affliction, their abundant joy and their extreme poverty have overflowed in a wealth of generosity on their part. For, as I can testify, they voluntarily gave according to their means, and even beyond their means, begging us earnestly for the privilege of sharing in this ministry to the saints – and this, not merely as we expected; they gave themselves first to the Lord.

In this passage, Paul is commending the generosity of the Macedonian churches in helping the Christians in Jerusalem: Gentiles supporting Jews. The problem has arisen because early Jewish converts were then cut off from their relatives, business and from the temple. Although the early believers 'had all things in common', this evidently could not last forever. Thus Paul appeals to his churches to support their brothers and sisters in Christ. Today we are perhaps even more aware that our faith is a worldwide one and our 'family' therefore international. We have a responsibility to be aware of, and to support the needs of, those we may not see or know personally but who are nonetheless our siblings.

The generosity of this particular church is amazing. Being poor themselves, how did they do it? But isn't this often the way? It is often those with limited resources who are more generous with what they have – perhaps because they understand all too well what it means to be forced to live with deprivation. For the Macedonians there is also another reason: they gave themselves first to the Lord.

This is becoming a familiar theme: the realisation that all we have, and are, belongs to God releases us then to release our 'possessions' as he prompts. And what a change of heart! This becomes not a duty but a pleasure; not a threat to our own well-being but a liberation; not condescension but privilege.

Lord, put on my heart fellow Christians for whom I should care and pray;
help me to release my resources as far as possible,
trusting in your faithfulness and provision. Amen

SHEILA WALKER

How much to keep?

'Beware of the scribes… They devour widows' houses and for the sake of appearance say long prayers. They will receive the greater condemnation.' He looked up and saw rich people putting their gifts into the treasury; he also saw a poor widow put in two small copper coins. He said, 'Truly I tell you, this poor widow has put in more than all of them; for all of them have contributed out of their abundance, but she out of her poverty has put in all she had to live on.'

It is easy for us to take the account of the widow's mite as a stand-alone story of whole-hearted, trustful giving. But we should also take account of the context, as Jesus is seeking here not only to honour her generosity but to compare it with the hypocritical self-seeking of the supposedly religious.

The scribes who, of all people, should have understood what kind of Messiah they should expect are blinded by their addiction to the outward trimmings of office, seeing nothing wrong in cheating the poor and making do with an outward show of piety. It is perhaps largely thanks to them that the widow has only these two very small coins left, and these she gives not out of obligation as some form of temple tax, but freely.

Considering our own expenditure, some will evidently be from obligation – mortgages, bills and so on – and some will be free will – gifts for friends and family, maybe other charitable giving. Do our churches advocate a certain level of giving, a tithe of some kind? How should we respond: obligation or love? True, our motives are usually mixed, and it isn't helpful to beat ourselves up too much about this, but taking stock from time to time can be salutary.

It is evident from this incident that God is not concerned about the amount of our giving but, as has often been pointed out, what remains after it has been given.

Lord, help me to see all my expenditure as you see it. Where I have obligations, may I discharge them cheerfully and with gratitude; where resources remain, may I give or invest them with wisdom and love, through the inspiration of your Holy Spirit. Amen

SHEILA WALKER

Mixed motives?

'Beware of practising your piety before others in order to be seen by them; for then you have no reward from your Father in heaven. So whenever you give alms, do not sound a trumpet before you, as the hypocrites do in the synagogues and in the streets, so that they may be praised by others. Truly I tell you, they have received their reward. But when you give alms, do not let your left hand know what your right hand is doing, so that your alms may be done in secret; and your Father who sees in secret will reward you.'

The sermon on the mount has a well-earned reputation for cutting to the quick, exposing the attitude of our heart which underlies our actions, however they may appear on the surface. Usually this is a salutary safeguard against pride, a reminder that we are forever flawed creatures dependent on the grace of God. Almsgiving was thought by some Jews to atone for sin, but outward action without right attitude brings only the superficial 'reward' of recognition by others. The courts of heaven are not impressed, and nothing of eternal value is achieved.

There are many stories along the lines of the bishop who skipped Sunday service in order to play golf, scored a hole in one but then couldn't tell anyone about it. But how much greater the temptation to tell when the action is one to provoke not guilt but a legitimate sense of satisfaction – and there are so many ways of dropping a subtle hint! On the other hand, we read of those whose families never knew the extent of their relative's giving until their death.

We can tie ourselves in knots over the conundrum that, if we know God will reward our secret giving, then that in turn becomes an equally unworthy motive. This should surely not be a reason not to do as he commands and give discreetly, just an added reminder to seek his grace to transform our hearts.

Lord, help me to be content to be silent: not to seek the praise of others,
but rather to wait on your 'Well done, good and faithful servant',
knowing that this too will be from your grace. Amen

SHEILA WALKER

Give us a chance

'Remember the Lord, who is great and awesome, and fight for your kin, your sons, your daughters, your wives, and your homes.' When our enemies heard that their plot was known to us, and that God had frustrated it, we all returned to the wall, each to his work. From that day on, half of my servants worked on construction, and half held the spears, shields, bows and body-armour; and the leaders posted themselves behind the whole house of Judah, who were building the wall.'

Nehemiah has been called by God to oversee the rebuilding of the walls of Jerusalem after the wholesale destruction of the city by the Babylonians in 587BC. Artaxerxes has given permission, so the opposition is more by infiltration and terrorism. Nehemiah's wise response is a call to solidarity: a sharing of resources not only in the material sense of ensuring that all have a means of defence, but also recognising that shared responsibility and shared working leads to mutual encouragement and the raising of morale. Emotional and psychological sharing is equally – at times more – important, not least in this case where it is a more subtle kind of attack they are facing.

Nehemiah begins by reminding his people of the greatness of their Lord: trust in him is the necessary foundation for all they will need to do. Just as they will need to depend on the Lord, their families are depending on them; this is not just some great national project but one in which they have a personal stake. The new wall will be a shared resource, one which they can truly 'own'. They will have experienced both investment and return.

We mentioned earlier the need, when considering 'sharing', to remember the importance of dignity and mutuality: for people to be able to do, as well as being done to; to work, as well as to receive support; to give, as well as to receive. It often seems today that people either have no work or are working insanely long hours. How might we tackle this destructive pattern?

Lord, help us to learn from Nehemiah's skilful leadership
in sharing vision, giving opportunity, providing work and building
not only walls but community. Amen

SHEILA WALKER

Giving ourselves away

A soft answer turns away wrath, but a harsh word stirs up anger. The tongue of the wise dispenses knowledge, but the mouths of fools pour out folly... Without counsel, plans go wrong, but with many advisers they succeed. To make an apt answer is a joy to anyone, and a word in season, how good it is!

Sharing, as we have said, is not only about material resources; it's about sharing ourselves – our expertise, our wisdom, our sympathy, our encouragement, our love.

With expertise, there may be times when it is right to safeguard 'intellectual property', but in terms of personal relationships, God-given expertise is to be shared as generously as any other kind of wealth we may have.

With wisdom, we are instructed to seek 'wisdom from above' (James 3:17), which is pure, peaceable, gentle, full of mercy and good fruits; as believers, we are to be open to the leading of the Holy Spirit and his inspiration. Problems which appear to defy human resolution may need the God-given 'wisdom of Solomon': proverbial for a reason, and surely available in every area of life, practical as well as spiritual, business as well as pleasure.

'Death and life are in the power of the tongue' (Proverbs 18:21), and James reinforces the fact that we should watch our words carefully, because they do indeed have power to hurt as well as to heal. It's not just a case of biting back words of criticism or sarcasm, but actively seeking to share words of encouragement and faith, as well as God's grace to transform the negative elements in our hearts and minds.

Emotionally, too, we are to share ourselves. Are we willing to be vulnerable? Sometimes sharing our own weaknesses and failures can help build understanding and trust. Being alongside someone who is struggling or hurting can be more important than providing 'answers', though it depends on our having confidence that someone greater is holding us both safely.

Lord, may we be humble enough to seek the support of others and secure enough in your love to make ourselves vulnerable in coming alongside those in need, through the indwelling of your Holy Spirit. Amen

SHEILA WALKER

Gaining from pain

Blessed be the God and Father of our Lord Jesus Christ, the Father of mercies and the God of all consolation, who consoles us in all our affliction, so that we may be able to console those who are in any affliction with the consolation with which we ourselves are consoled by God. For just as the sufferings of Christ are abundant for us, so also our consolation is abundant through Christ. If we are being afflicted it is for your consolation and salvation; if we are being consoled, it is for your consolation, which you experience when you patiently endure the same sufferings that we are also suffering.

Suffering may come because of one's own sin, because of one's faith or simply because we live in a broken world. Paul's words here are born out of his own considerable suffering because of his Christian witness, and his experience of God's consolation and deliverance. Suffering for one's faith is unique and often inevitable for the believer, but so too is their access to divine help. Christians should, therefore, be especially aware of the suffering of their fellow believers across the world and ready to share with them whatever practical, emotional or spiritual resources they have.

Here, the ever-present question of why there is suffering receives, if not an answer, a helpful response. Our own suffering helps us understand the suffering of others, so that, as we seek and experience God's help in responding, wisdom and healing can be shared with them. It may be sad but true that we need the shock of a pandemic, a hurricane or a recession to trigger our imagination and compassion, which in turn may lead to changes not only in our own personal response but in government policy and provision.

So how do we respond to our own times of affliction? It is easy to simply focus on surviving them without too much grumbling or burdening other people, but maybe we should also be asking, 'Where is God in all this? How is he present? What is he wanting me to learn?' We may then become more aware of the nature of that consolation we have to pass on to fellow-sufferers.

Lord, may it be so. Amen

SHEILA WALKER

Jesus every time

'Then the righteous will answer him, "Lord, when was it that we saw you hungry and gave you food, or thirsty and gave you something to drink? And when was it that we saw you a stranger and welcomed you, or naked and gave you clothing? And when was it that we saw you sick or in prison and visited you?" And the king will answer them, "Truly I tell you, just as you did it to one of the least of these who are members of my family, you did it to me."'

It isn't always easy to 'see Christ' in other people, especially those we know only through news reports or who, on the other hand, are too close for comfort – the difficult neighbour, the so-called fellow Christian who should know better. Yet we know it is true that we all bear the image of Christ, and it is this that we should recognise and seek to encourage, so that it may be truly transformational. If only! If only we could indeed see one another in this light and respond accordingly, how many of our tensions, how much of our disunity would vanish overnight.

It has always been a humbling wake-up call for me to remember that in an institution where Mother Teresa cared for the poor and dying, over each bed were the words 'the body of Christ'. These were people with little earthly beauty or apparent merit: the destitute, sick and dying. But here was the reminder to offer them care fit for a king, service due to a God.

What does this tell us about sharing resources? Something, perhaps, about not always being too calculating, too parsimonious, too judgemental about how deserving – or not – someone may be? If the recipient is always, in some sense, Jesus, then nothing less than excellence is truly fitting. This is not to decry the need for wisdom: rather to beware of the temptation to rationalise away what may be divine promptings to love extravagantly.

Paul writes to the Colossians of 'Christ in you, the hope of glory'.
Lord Jesus, help us not only to know it in theory but to discern
your presence in one another, allowing your Spirit to transform
our response. Amen

SHEILA WALKER

Refuseniks?

'At midnight there was a shout, "Look! Here is the bridegroom! Come out to meet him." Then all those bridesmaids got up and trimmed their lamps. The foolish said to the wise, "Give us some of your oil, for our lamps are going out." But the wise replied, "No! there will not be enough for you and for us; you had better go to the dealers and buy some for yourselves." And while they went to buy it, the bridegroom came, and those who were ready went with him into the wedding banquet; and the door was shut.'

Is it ever right *not* to share? This parable is admittedly not primarily about sharing, but being prepared. But it raises the question. It shows that there are some things we cannot borrow or acquire from others. We cannot, for example, trade off someone else's faith. There can be an ambiguity when someone asks us to pray for them – of course, we will, and gladly, but it should not be an excuse for them not also to seek God for themselves, to discover or deepen their relationship with him.

On a more material level, for some people it may be more appropriate to support a homeless charity rather than give to an individual, but doubts about how that individual might spend the money should not excuse us from responding to their need, and the needs of others. Obviously, too, we will not support appeals about which we may have ethical concerns, taking care not to be unduly influenced by the spirit of the times, but to bring such issues before God, asking for discernment.

Another potentially grey area is that of advice. A good counsellor will rarely give direction; rather, they will enable the person to see their situation clearly and come to a wise decision for themselves, which they will then own. It can be tempting to say, 'If I were you, I would definitely do…', but sharing wisdom in such situations is often better expressed by asking key questions or providing relevant information.

Lord, help us to know that we are not at the mercy of everyone who asks something of us. May your Holy Spirit show us when it is right to hold back: to pause, pray and seek your wisdom. Amen

SHEILA WALKER

The limits of growth

Though the fig tree does not blossom, and no fruit is on the vines; though the produce of the olive fails and the fields yield no food; though the flock is cut off from the fold and there is no herd in the stalls, yet I will rejoice in the Lord; I will exult in the God of my salvation. God, the Lord, is my strength; he makes my feet like the feet of a deer, and makes me tread upon the heights.

Little is known of Habakkuk, a prophet writing around 600BC of God's intention to use the Chaldeans to bring judgement on his sinful people. Terrible though that judgement may be, however, Habakkuk is able to conclude his prophecy with these triumphant, faith-filled words, based on his confidence that even in judgement God will, somehow, remember mercy, enabling him to walk with the sure-footedness of a deer even through the most difficult times and places.

One of the most common objections to faith is that natural disasters of all kinds occur, leaving many at the mercy of flood and famine, earthquake and drought. Today, the situation is exacerbated by our own despoiling of our environment for commercial gain, often at the expense of indigenous communities. While the efforts of aid agencies help to mitigate the effects of irresponsible exploitation, hard decisions need to be taken at the government level if our planet is to be able to continue to resource its growing population.

Personal trust in God, such as Habakkuk's, looks very different if you live in Mali rather than Mayfair. Earth's resources are limited, and their distribution is hugely unequal. Depending on where we live, how should we respond to our global situation? Yes, we are called to trust God, but are we also called to act? To lobby? To pray? To modify our own lifestyle? To give?

Lord, raise my awareness of those places where there is indeed no fruit on the vine and no bread on the table. Help me to weep with those who weep, and to ask what can I do and how can I help. Help me to remember, too, my need to trust at all times and, like Paul, to rest content, in times of need as well as of plenty. Amen

SHEILA WALKER

Rivers

 I have never been one for geography, having suffered extreme boredom during school lessons carrying out traffic surveys or colouring in pictures of an oxbow lake. Consequently there is a huge gap in my knowledge about rivers – so don't expect enlightenment in that area from these reflections!

I do have, however, a deep experience of rivers, from swimming in them, living alongside them and, most significantly, walking along their banks on my many pilgrim journeys in this country and further afield. River courses make easy walking – towns are built near to them, and navigation is simple if their route is followed. In this country, rivers often lead to ancient ports, launching places for pilgrims eager to travel to Rome, Santiago de Compostela or Jerusalem.

As I have followed their courses, I have appreciated how much rivers affect the landscape, both natural and built, and how great are the gifts that these sources of running water bestow upon all of creation. Rivers must not be taken for granted; they need careful management to remain clear and clean. They should not be underestimated; flooding and drought carry equal threat to the well-being of creation. Part of our role as stewards of God's creation is to tend our rivers so that they may in turn maintain our communities.

The Bible begins and ends with a river – one flows out of Eden to nourish the world so that it can be tilled by the first of God's children, and one flows from the throne of God to fill our hearts and souls with life and love. In between we glimpse the life-giving properties of water, both physical and spiritual, and learn how God's care for his people extends to all parts of our lives. Rivers are places of encounter and healing, of meeting and praying; they are metaphors and symbols, reminding us of the flow of life from and towards our God.

O glide, fair stream! For ever so;
Thy quiet soul on all bestowing,
Till all our minds for ever flow,
As thy deep waters now are flowing.

'Lines Written Near Richmond, Upon the Thames at Evening', by William Wordsworth

SALLY WELCH

The first river

The Lord God planted a garden in Eden, toward the east, where he placed the man whom he had formed. The Lord God caused every tree that is both beautiful and suitable for food to spring up out of the ground. The tree of life was also in the middle of the garden, along with the tree of the knowledge of good and evil. A river flows from Eden to water the garden, and from there it divides, becoming four branches.

One glorious summer I was part of a group leading a pilgrimage along the section of the Thames Path which flowed through Oxford Diocese. Over the ten days of the expedition we were joined by over 100 people, including four bishops. We walked together, prayed together and marvelled at the landscape which unfolded before us, all of it shaped by the River Thames as it flowed through towns and villages, green spaces and industrial sites, changing and yet never changing, constantly moving along an age-old route.

The creation story in Genesis 2 includes a river – water is a fundamental of life and no garden would flourish without a plentiful supply. But the river in Eden does more than simply enable the garden to grow – it flows out beyond the borders, dividing into four branches. These branches, we are told, become the rivers Pishon, Gihon, Tigris and Euphrates. The Tigris and the Euphrates are real, geographically certified rivers; the others have been identified variously with the Nile, the Ganges and the Sefīd-Rūd. All of these are important, significant rivers, which nourish the landscape of the Middle East. The river of the creation story and the real-life rivers are indistinguishable, flowing from one to another.

So too can the river of our faith, our belief in the creator God, the river of our minds and souls, flow outward into our everyday lives, informing and transforming our words and actions so that they nourish and support not only our life but the lives of those around us.

Lord, let me be a conduit for your loving words of creation.
Let my words and actions support and sustain the lives of others,
nourishing both myself and those around me.

SALLY WELCH

Eternally flowing

Look! There is a river whose streams make the city of God rejoice, even the Holy Place of the Most High. Since God is in her midst, she will not be shaken. God will help her at the break of dawn. The nations roared; the kingdoms were shaken. His voice boomed; the earth melts. The Lord of the heavenly armies is with us; our refuge is the God of Jacob.

There is a river at the bottom of the hill which I can see from my study window. It is the Evenlode, a tributary of the Thames. Geographically it's unremarkable – it rises near Moreton-in-Marsh, flows for about 45 miles through the Cotswolds then joins the Thames just north of Oxford.

To me, however, it is more than that. For seven years it has been part of my landscape, as it has bubbled and chattered through the valley, hosting ducks and wildlife, the sunlight dancing off its ripples. I have seen it in times of drought when it has shrunk to a shallow film of water just covering the riverbed, while ducks and water birds wander disconsolately among the stones, picking up a few starved fish. I have seen it when it has been in full flood and the fields on either side of the bank have become part of the waterway, with only the branches of trees showing where land ends and river begins. It is always the same, and it is endlessly different as it reflects the clouds and skies and is stirred up by wind or shaken by rainstorms.

So too is the presence of God in our lives. His being is constant and eternal – the river that never runs dry, bringing refreshment and renewal, causing us to rejoice in his loving care for us. We may experience him in different ways; our awareness of his action in our lives may grow or diminish according to the state of our relationship with him, how closely we are walking with him. But even when we fear his absence, it is only our blindness which prevents us from seeing.

Eternal God, help me to trust that since you are in our midst,
we will not be shaken.

SALLY WELCH

Singing songs

There we sat down and cried – by the rivers of Babylon – as we remembered Zion. On the willows there we hung our harps, for it was there that our captors asked us for songs and our torturers demanded joy from us, 'Sing us one of the songs about Zion!' How are we to sing the song of the Lord on foreign soil?

The experience of the pandemic shook my parish. Our security was shattered as those things upon which we had relied – access to healthcare, shops open for long hours, the companionship of friends and neighbours – disappeared or became radically altered. Our churches were closed, and so were our cafes, pubs, restaurants and gathering places. Suddenly our environment was unfamiliar and even hostile as the threat of infection lurked with every encounter.

In that strange land many of us questioned our ability to 'sing the song of the Lord'. How were we to worship if our buildings were closed? How could we serve our neighbours if they had shut themselves behind their front doors, never to emerge? Of course, new ways of worship did emerge as we 'went online', made phone calls, delivered 'Easter in a bag'. We served our neighbours as we did their shopping, collected their parcels, arranged transportation to vaccination centres. But the old ways remained precious, too, some of them gaining in significance even as new trends emerged.

Just as the exiles in Babylon found solace in the rivers of their strange new country, reminding them of their homeland and encouraging them to look downstream to new possibilities and future destinations, so we can discover again the strength which lies behind the traditions of centuries. The power of silence, the comfort of song, the revelations of Bible study, the resilience-building of fasting – all these gifts from former times can serve to support and sustain us when we enter into new territory, whether that territory is unfamiliar only to us or whether the route is one as yet untravelled by humanity.

Lord of all the world, help us to find you when we travel through unfamiliar territory. Guide us as we explore strange landscapes and lead us to the signposts of your love.

SALLY WELCH

Wild swimming

'Look at Zion, city of our festivals! Your eyes will see Jerusalem, an undisturbed abode, an immovable tent; its stakes will never be pulled up, nor will any of its ropes be broken. But there the Lord in majesty will be for us our source of broad rivers and streams, where no galley with oars can go, where no stately ship can sail. For the Lord is our judge, and the Lord is our lawgiver; and the Lord is our king, and it is he who will save us.'

I learnt how to swim in a river. I think this was perhaps because my mother learnt to swim in the sea, making her way across the small bay near her childhood home, often unwittingly out of her depth and usually rather cold. After such an experience I suspect she felt the normal swimming pool plus instructor was somehow cheating and that nature was the best teacher.

So, keeping my mouth firmly shut and my shoes on, I first paddled then swam in rivers and lakes in this country and abroad, and I have never lost my enthusiasm for what is now called 'wild swimming'. To submerge oneself in water when the sun is beating down overhead, feeling the strength of the current, the changes in temperature, to float idly downstream and battle one's way back up is a source of great joy.

The image of God as a source of broad rivers and streams, offering us intense refreshment, challenge and delight can resonate not just with those of us who plunge right into rivers and lakes, but for all of us who take delight in feeling fresh water trickling through our fingers or in dipping our toes into ponds and streams. This metaphor is made more powerful by the sense of protection we are given in the invulnerability of the rivers and streams – we cannot be attacked by our enemies, as they cannot reach us if we are immersed in the Lord. We can put our whole trust in him alone as he surrounds us with the power of his love.

Lord, let the refreshing waters of your love surround us and protect us. Help us to put our faith in you, our Saviour.

SALLY WELCH

'Do not be afraid'

But now this is what the Lord says, the one who created you, Jacob, the one who formed you, Israel: 'Do not be afraid, because I've redeemed you. I've called you by name; you are mine. When you pass through the waters, I'll be with you; and through the rivers, they won't sweep over you. When you walk through fire you won't be scorched, and the flame won't set you ablaze.'

How interesting that yesterday's reading used the metaphor of rivers and streams to convey an image of God's protection, whereas today the image of water is frightening and overwhelming. There is something about a large body of water which conveys so powerfully a feeling of helplessness in the face of a threat. We imagine huge, rolling waves crashing down over us, knocking us off balance and sending us spiralling into panic as we struggle to find our feet and to breathe amid the noise and the violence of a storm-filled sea or a river in full flood.

Some of the events of our lives feel much like that – a wild, unstoppable force, against which we have no power or control, which turns upside down all that is normal and safe and sends us to a place where nothing is familiar, full of fear and suffering.

Then we would do well to remember these words, to remember that first brave journey of the children of Israel through the waters of the Red Sea, stepping out along the path though the waters piled up either side, placing their trust in the God who led them safely through, not permitting them to be overwhelmed or swept away. Then we can go forth in faith, putting our hope in our redeemer Jesus Christ, who suffered all things for our sakes, and whose love surrounds us daily, no matter where we are or what we are experiencing.

Through waves and clouds and storms
his power will clear thy way:
wait thou his time; the darkest night
shall end in brightest day.
(John Wesley, 1703–91)

SALLY WELCH

'Did you see all this?'

Then, as he was bringing me back along the river bank, he asked me, 'Son of Man, did you see all of this?' As we were coming back, I was amazed to see that there were many, many trees lining both banks of the river… **'Lining each side of the river banks, all sorts of species of fruit trees will be growing. Their leaves will never wither and their fruit will never fail. They will bear fruit every month, because the water that nourishes them will be flowing from the sanctuary. Their fruit will be for food and their leaves will contain substances that promote healing.'**

Ezekiel was both fortunate and unfortunate in his life as a prophet. He was vindicated in his work, as his prophecy came true, but unfortunately the prophecy was one of disaster and exile. Like many of his people, Ezekiel lost his home, his role in the temple and his country, as he was forced to begin a new life in a foreign country.

Tasked with bringing hope to a people who had not only lost their homeland but whose very concept of God was threatened – since God and the temple, the promised land and its children were all bound up together – Ezekiel shares pictures of a future filled with promise. Life can be breathed into old bones, in that famous image in Ezekiel 37 ('a great many bones… bones that were very dry', v. 2, NIV).

At the end of the book, Ezekiel is taken by God to the city of Jerusalem, the city which the prophet left in ruins, but which has now been rebuilt on a more glorious scale than ever. God shows him a magnificent temple, which is described in lavish detail. And at the heart of the temple is the river, which flows through the building and out, providing a source of nourishment and healing for all who live in the holy city.

Christians find nourishment not in bricks and mortar, however grand, but in the living temple, Jesus Christ. If we open our hearts to him, then his love and healing will flow through us and out to the world.

Lord Jesus Christ, let your living waters quench my thirst.

SALLY WELCH

Walking the walk

'I hate – I despise – your festival days, and your solemn convocations stink. And if you send up burnt offerings to me as well as your grain offerings, I will not accept them, nor will I consider your peace offerings of fattened cattle. Spare me your noisy singing – I will not listen to your musical instruments. But let justice roll on like many waters, and right-eousness like an ever-flowing river.'

Amos wasn't a professional prophet – he was simply a shepherd. He didn't live in Jerusalem, but in the Judean hill country to the south. However, he did witness the gradual slide into corruption and decline which was Israel's fate during the second half of the reign of King Jeroboam, leading eventually to the fall of Jerusalem in 722BC. Amos witnessed it and proclaimed against it – the chosen people of God were not following his ways and needed to be told so.

A first reading of these verses suggests that Amos is calling to account the people's religious practices – festivals, sacrifices and even the playing of music seem to be no longer acceptable. However, it is important not to miss the point, which is not against rites and rituals as such, but when the impulse of praise and worship, of following God's commands, does not flow outwards from the temple and into everyday life. However excellent the action inside the temple, it is scorned by God if it is not mirrored in the action outside – justice and righteousness, respect for all people, serving each other and helping the poor.

Our faith is not a Sunday-morning faith – it is not confined to liturgy and doctrine, although our times of gathering together are a vital part of who we are as the body of Christ. Christianity is a Monday-to-Sunday way of life, when the refreshment, encouragement, teaching and fellowship we receive when we gather together flows outwards into the wider community and expresses itself in loving service to all those in need. And not just on an intermittent basis either, but like 'many waters', an 'ever-flowing river' – expansive and continuous.

Lord, help me to live out my beliefs in action underpinned by praise.

SALLY WELCH

The gift of the Spirit

Then Jesus came from Galilee to the Jordan to be baptised by John. But John tried to stop him, saying, 'I need to be baptised by you, and are you coming to me?' But Jesus answered him, 'Let it be this way for now, because this is the proper way for us to fulfil all righteousness.' At this, he permitted him to be baptised. When Jesus had been baptised, he immediately came up out of the water. Suddenly, the heavens opened up for him, and he saw the Spirit of God descending like a dove and coming to rest on him. Then a voice from heaven said, 'This is my Son, whom I love. I am pleased with him!'

Of course, Jesus did not need to be baptised. He was 'without sin', the one who came to rescue us from the consequences of our sins. So why did he step down into the water and allow John to plunge him into the depths of the River Jordan? To show us the way – simply that. By living among us, Jesus showed us how to be more fully human. By sharing our lives, he demonstrated how we might have more life.

Most baptisms nowadays involve less water than an entire river immersing our bodies, washing us clean literally as well as symbolically. But it doesn't need much – just enough to flow over us, reminding us of that first baptism of water and Spirit, offering each one of us the path back to life through forgiveness of our sins, opening the way for all of us to repent and be forgiven.

And, filled as we are with the gift of the Spirit, given to all those who are baptised, we become children of God, able to share with all his children his great love. The words addressed to Christ as he emerges from the water, filled with the Spirit, are for all of us to hear – words of affirmation, of delight, of acceptance of all we are and hope for all we can be.

Repeat God's loving words to yourself. Allow yourself to be open to his Spirit, and believe in his words. And then live as if you believe.

SALLY WELCH

Thirst-quenching

On the last and most important day of the festival, Jesus stood up and shouted, 'If anyone is thirsty, let him come to me and drink! The one who believes in me, as the Scripture has said, will have rivers of living water flowing from his heart.' Now he said this about the Spirit, whom those who were believing in him were to receive, because the Spirit was not yet present and Jesus had not yet been glorified.

The festival referred to here is the Feast of Tabernacles, or Sukkot, one of the major events in Jewish religious life. Those who could would travel to Jerusalem and join together in celebration. Originally intended as a harvest thanksgiving, by the time of Christ it had been extended to include God's gracious provision for his people during their wilderness wandering. As part of the rituals, water was drawn from the Pool of Siloam and carried along the pilgrim road to the temple, where it was poured out as prayers were said.

Jesus takes part in the celebrations; he joins in the thanksgiving for God's unwavering love for his children and the trust in that provision in future years. But he offers something more – the opportunity to share in the 'living water', which is the Spirit of God, allowing it to flow in and through each one of us, should we just approach the source of the water and accept and drink.

John reminds us that those hearing Jesus' words of promise had not yet received the Spirit, as Jesus' work on earth had not been completed. But the anticipation is evident. The invitation is open and inclusive of all. And the living water will flow from the hearts of those who drink, out into the world, refreshing all who come into contact with the outpouring of God's love.

I heard the voice of Jesus say,
'Behold, I freely give
the living water, thirsty one;
stoop down and drink and live.'
I came to Jesus, and I drank
of that life-giving stream.
My thirst was quenched, my soul revived,
and now I live in him.
(Horatius Bonar, 1808–89)

SALLY WELCH

Lessons for living

On the Sabbath day, we went out the city gate and walked along the river, where we thought there was a place of prayer. We sat down and began talking to the women who had gathered there. A woman named Lydia, from the city of Thyatira, a dealer in purple goods, was listening to us. She was a worshipper of God, and the Lord opened her heart to listen carefully to what was being said by Paul. When she and her family were baptised, she urged us, 'If you are convinced that I am a believer in the Lord, come and stay at my home.' And she continued to insist that we do so.

This is such a slight story, easy to miss among the stories of storms and persecution, lives risked, miracles delivered, crowds converted. But it contains within it some important principles of mission and Christian community.

It is the Sabbath, and Paul, being a Jew as well as a Christian, seeks somewhere to pray. There wasn't a synagogue in Philippi, so he looked for a gathering of people to pray with. Wherever he was, whatever he was doing, Paul kept up his rhythm of prayer. Travelling was not an excuse, nor was being a stranger in town; as a priority, he looked for a community with whom to gather and pray. If Paul doesn't remain in the Lord, how will he carry out the Lord's tasks properly?

The river isn't a synagogue, but that doesn't matter to Paul – he doesn't need buildings or music, complicated rituals and processions, just a community. The people are women – at that time a most insignificant sector of the population, often powerless and many dependent on men to survive. That doesn't matter either – whoever they are, whatever their status, Paul will share in their worship. After praying, Paul speaks, and the women listen. He has already demonstrated that he is willing to join their community, so he speaks as one among them. Lydia is baptised and offers hospitality, which is received gratefully and gracefully by Paul.

A rhythm of prayer, inclusive community, generous hospitality – three essentials of Christian life demonstrated in one brief episode.

Lord, help me live out your truth in all things.

SALLY WELCH

The river of life

Then the angel showed me the river of the water of life, as clear as crystal. It was flowing from the throne of God and the lamb. Between the city street and the river, the tree of life was visible from each side. It produced twelve kinds of fruit, each month having its own fruit. The leaves of the tree are for the healing of the nations. There will no longer be any curse. The throne of God and the lamb will be in the city. His servants will worship him and see his face, and his name will be on their foreheads. There will be no more night, and they will not need any light from lamps or the sun because the Lord God will shine on them. They will rule forever and ever.

What a wonderful, poetic, encouraging, inspiring piece of writing! Written by a visionary with a heart for his people who are suffering appalling persecution, in daily terror of death, this description of the new Jerusalem must surely serve as an encouragement for all those who are experiencing times of difficulty or sorrow.

The city of God, where the natural world and humankind clearly live in harmony with each other, is a place full of light and joy. At its heart is God and the lamb, and from its heart flows the river of the water of life. It is this which nurtures the city, enabling growth and healing. It is from this river that we are invited to drink, as we share in God's kingdom.

Caught between the now and the not yet, held in tension between the eternal triumph of goodness over evil and the evil which surrounds all of us as we live out our lives on this flawed and fractured planet, we can gaze at this picture in awe and wonder. We can be certain of our hope for the future, and look for the time when the 'old order of things has passed away' (Revelation 21:4, NIV). We must hold in our hearts this picture of the redemption of the world, allowing it to illumine our daily lives and shine forth in our words and deeds.

'Amen! Come, Lord Jesus!' (Revelation 22:20).

SALLY WELCH

Become a Friend of BRF
and give regularly
to support our ministry

We help people of all ages to grow in faith

We encourage and support individual Christians and churches as they serve and resource the changing spiritual needs of communities today.

Through **Anna Chaplaincy** we're enabling churches to provide spiritual care to older people

Through **Living Faith** we're nurturing faith and resourcing life-long discipleship

Through **Messy Church** we're helping churches to reach out to families

Through **Parenting for Faith** we're supporting parents as they raise their children in the Christian faith

Our ministry is only possible because of the generous support of individuals, churches, trusts and gifts in wills.

As we look to the future and make plans, **regular donations make a huge difference** in ensuring we can both start and finish projects well.

By becoming a Friend of BRF and giving regularly to our ministry you are partnering with us in the gospel and helping change lives.

How your gift makes a difference

£2
a month

Helps us to develop **Living Faith** resources to use in care homes and communities

£10
a month

Helps us to support churches running the **Parenting for Faith** course and stand alongside parents

£5
a month

Helps us to support **Messy Church** volunteers and resource and grow the wider network

£20
a month

Helps us to resource **Anna Chaplaincy** and improve spiritual care for older people

 How to become a Friend of BRF

Set up a Direct Debit donation at **brf.org.uk/donate** or find out how to set up a Standing Order at **brf.org.uk/friends**

Contact the fundraising team

Email: **giving@brf.org.uk**
Tel: +44 (0)1235 462305
Post: Fundraising team, BRF, 15 The Chambers, Vineyard, Abingdon OX14 3FE

Good to know

If you have any questions, or if you want to change your regular donation or stop giving in the future, do get in touch.

Registered with

FR

FUNDRAISING
REGULATOR

I would like to make a donation to support BRF.
Please use my gift for:

☐ Where it is most needed   ☐ Anna Chaplaincy   ☐ Living Faith
☐ Messy Church   ☐ Parenting for Faith

Title	First name/initials	Surname
Address		
		Postcode
Email		
Telephone		
Signature		Date

Our ministry is only possible because of the generous support of individuals, churches, trusts and gifts in wills.

giftaid it   You can add an extra 25p to every £1 you give.

Please treat as Gift Aid donations all qualifying gifts of money made

☐ today,   ☐ in the past four years,   ☐ and in the future.

I am a UK taxpayer and understand that if I pay less Income Tax and/or Capital Gains Tax in the current tax year than the amount of Gift Aid claimed on all my donations, it is my responsibility to pay any difference.

☐ My donation does not qualify for Gift Aid.

Please notify BRF if you want to cancel this Gift Aid declaration, change your name or home address, or no longer pay sufficient tax on your income and/or capital gains.

Please complete other side of form ➡

SHARING OUR VISION – MAKING A ONE-OFF GIFT

Please accept my gift of:

☐ £2 ☐ £5 ☐ £10 ☐ £20 Other £ [＿＿＿＿＿]

by (*delete as appropriate*):

☐ Cheque/Charity Voucher payable to 'BRF'

☐ MasterCard/Visa/Debit card/Charity card

Name on card

Card no. [＿][＿][＿][＿] [＿][＿][＿][＿] [＿][＿][＿][＿] [＿][＿][＿][＿]

Expires end [M][M] [Y][Y] Security code[*] [＿][＿][＿]

[*]Last 3 digits on the reverse of the card

Signature   Date

☐ I would like to leave a gift to BRF in my will.
Please send me further information.

For help or advice regarding making a gift, please contact
our fundraising team +44 (0)1235 462305

Your privacy

We will use your personal data to process this transaction.
From time to time we may send you information about
the work of BRF that we think may be of interest to you.
Our privacy policy is available at **brf.org.uk/privacy**.
Please contact us if you wish to discuss your mailing
preferences.

Registered with

FR

FUNDRAISING
REGULATOR

 Please complete other side of form

Please return this form to 'Freepost BRF'
No other address information or stamp is needed

BRF

Bible Reading Fellowship is a charity (233280) and company limited by
guarantee (301324), registered in England and Wales

Reading *New Daylight* in a group

SALLY WELCH

I am aware that although some of you cherish the moments of quiet during the day which enable you to read and reflect on the passages we offer you in *New Daylight*, other readers prefer to study in small groups, to enable conversation and discussion and the sharing of insights. With this in mind, here are some ideas for discussion starters within a study group. Some of the questions are generic and can be applied to any set of contributions within this issue; others are specific to certain sets of readings. I hope they generate some interesting reflections and conversations!

General discussion starters

These can be used for any study series within this issue. Remember there are no right or wrong answers – these questions are simply to enable a group to engage in conversation.

- What do you think is the main idea or theme of the author in this series? Do you think they succeeded in communicating this to you, or were you more interested in the side issues?

- Have you had any experience of the issues that are raised in the study? How have they affected your life?

- What evidence does the author use to support their ideas? Do they use personal observations and experience, facts, quotations from other authorities? Which appeals to you most?

- Does the author make a 'call to action'? Is that call realistic and achievable? Do you think their ideas will work in the secular world?

- Can you identify specific passages that struck you personally – as interesting, profound, difficult to understand or illuminating?

- Did you learn something new reading this series? Will you think differently about some things, and if so, what are they?

Questions for specific series

Desert spirituality (Veronica Zundel)

'Sailors beginning a voyage set the sails and look for a favourable wind, and later they meet a contrary wind… They do not throw the cargo overboard or abandon ship; they wait a while and struggle against the storm until they can set a direct course again' (Syncletica).

- What do you understand by the term 'desert spirituality'? Does it differ from Veronica's?
- Which aspects of this type of spiritual practice are appealing to you? How might you incorporate them into your prayer life?

Celebration (Lucy Moore)

- How do you feel about all-age worship? What is it like in your church? How might it be improved?
- All Jesus' words and actions are inclusive. How might your own words and behaviour become more inclusive?
- Who are the excluded in your daily experience? Have they changed at all since Jesus' time?

Standing still (Sally Welch)

- What has been your experience of 'living in the moment'?
- How easy is it for you to find God in the moment?
- How might the techniques of Christian mindfulness help you not to be so anxious or regretful?

Rivers (Sally Welch)

Rivers can be both delightful and dangerous, restorative and challenging. Faith too can be all of these things. Which parts of your Christian practice do you find restorative, and which challenging? How healthy is the balance of these things in your life? Should you be thinking of ways to alter the balance?

Meet the author: Louise Davis

What does your work at the Arthur Rank Centre involve?

I've been part of the team at the Arthur Rank Centre since 2016 and in that time my role has evolved significantly. I'm currently the training manager, responsible for overseeing and developing our training opportunities for rural church leaders, lay and ordained, from across the denominational spectrum. For five years I was the editor of our magazine, *Country Way*, and helped shape our Rural Mission Sunday initiative. Both were developed to create space for rural churches to tell their stories and challenge themselves to do new things to bless, support and encourage their communities.

For me, the common thread that runs through so much of the rural mission and ministry that we see and hear about at the Arthur Rank Centre is the extraordinary creativity and imagination that is at the heart of so many rural churches and their communities, and helping to tell those stories has been a huge privilege.

And what do you do in your spare time?

I'm the volunteer chaplain at Leicester City Football Club, working with their women's first team. I usually spend at least a day a week with the players and backroom staff, essentially loitering with intent. I'm the only Christian in the women's first team, and it's a huge privilege to – in a phrase I've used in my notes on the book of James – be God's hands and feet in that place. I'm also a trustee for Sports Chaplaincy UK, the charity which oversees my own chaplaincy role, and in my 'real' spare time I like to garden and read!

Who or what are your spiritual influences?

My early influences were the Christians in my immediate family – parents, grandparents and sisters – and the Baptist church family of which I was a part. Over the years my faith was shaped by the contemporary Christian music I listened to, the festivals I attended, the books I read.

Many of these reflected my own ethnic and cultural background and more recently I've been making a conscious effort to listen to voices that tell stories and share experiences very different to my own, and my faith continues to grow deeper and richer as a result.

Recommended reading

In *Grief Notes* Tony Horsfall charts the first year of his grief journey since the death of his wife from cancer. Month by month he tells the unfolding story of walking with and through loss, weaving this together with biblical teaching on grief and insights gained from grief counselling. With a poignant mix of honesty and humour, Tony shares the challenges of rebuilding his life and reflects on how he has seen God meet his needs as he wrestled with grieving in a time of lockdown and pandemic. The following is an edited extract taken from the first chapter of the book.

Grief Notes
Walking through loss
The first year after bereavement

Tony Horsfall

13 July

Evelyn passed away peacefully in the early hours of this morning. I had prayed with her last night before I left Cherry Trees, the care home where she was being nursed. Although at that stage she was not able to communicate much, at the end of my prayer she blurted out, 'Thank you, Jesus. You led me all the way.' These were the last words she spoke, and they gave me great assurance that she was ready to go home to be with Jesus.

The care home called me just after 2.00 am, but when I got there, she was gone. It was hard to see her lying there, lifeless, her skin cold and the colour of bone china. Even though expected, her death was still a shock. I packed her things and tidied her room as I waited for the undertaker to arrive. I spoke to my son Alistair in Australia, as I knew he would be awake.

Then, with great dignity, she was taken away, and I was alone. I will never see her again on this earth.

A time for everything

You may be familiar with the great passage in Ecclesiastes 3:1–11 with its 14 statements about life, realities that are as true now as when they were when first written centuries before Christ was born. It begins like this: 'There is a time for everything, and a season for every activity under the heavens' (v. 1). Then comes the first punch line, describing the most universal of life experiences, and it hits you hard in the stomach – 'A time to be born and a time to die' (v. 2). In a culture that likes to pretend that death is not real and can be avoided, we are pierced by the raw reality that there will come a moment in time when death touches every one of us.

Death is inevitable. There is a time to be born. There is a time to die. No one lives forever, and sooner or later we will become familiar with the reality that we – and those we love – are frail and finite creatures with a limited timespan on planet earth. We can celebrate births and birthdays with joy and gladness, but inevitably we shall also mourn the death of loved ones and grieve their passing with tears of sadness.

Grieving is painful, for as we read here there is also a time to weep (v. 4). Of course, we would prefer life to be all sunshine, every day filled with fun and laughter, but the shadow of death is never far away, especially as we get older. Grief is the price we pay for loving, and our tears reflect the pain we feel when we lose someone dear to us.

Grief is not permanent, however. We may never completely get over it, but we do come through it. 'There is a time to mourn and a time to dance' (v. 4). It may seem impossible when we are in the midst of grief to think that we could ever be happy again, but we will be. Slowly, with the passing of time and the brave work that grieving well requires of us, we will emerge into the brightness of a new day. Joy will return. That has to be our hope, for without such a prospect we may well stay submerged in the darkness of loss forever.

This truth gives us belief that we can find a way through our grief and come out the other side to live again. Yes, and even to dance once more!

To order a copy of this book, please use the order form opposite or visit **brfonline.org.uk**.

order

ne: **brfonline.org.uk**
phone: +44 (0)1865 319700
–Fri 9.30–17.00

Delivery times within the UK are normally 15 working days. Prices are correct at the time of going to press but may change without prior notice.

le	Price	Qty	Total
tic Prayer – Caught Up In Love	£12.99		
e People's Bible Commentary: Gospels and Acts (boxed set)	£39.99		
ef Notes	£8.99		

POSTAGE AND PACKING CHARGES			
r value	UK	Europe	Rest of world
er £7.00	£2.00	Available on request	Available on request
0–£29.99	£3.00		
00 and over	FREE		

Total value of books	
Postage and packing	
Donation*	
Total for this order	

* Please complete and return the Gift Aid declaration on page 143.

se complete in BLOCK CAPITALS

le .... First name/initials .... Surname...............................

dress..

.... Postcode ....

c. No. .... Telephone ....

nail...

ethod of payment

☐ Cheque (made payable to BRF) ☐ MasterCard / Visa

rd no. ☐☐☐☐ ☐☐☐☐ ☐☐☐☐ ☐☐☐☐ ☐☐☐☐

pires end ☐☐ ☐☐ Security code ☐☐☐ Last 3 digits on the reverse of the card

will use your personal data to process this order. From time to time we may send you information t the work of BRF. Please contact us if you wish to discuss your mailing preferences **brf.org.uk/privacy**

se return this form to:

15 The Chambers, Vineyard, Abingdon OX14 3FE | **enquiries@brf.org.uk**
erms and cancellation information, please visit **brfonline.org.uk/terms**.

Bible Reading Fellowship is a charity (233280) and company limited by guarantee (301324), registered in England and Wales

BRF needs you!

If you're one of our many thousands of regular *New Daylight* readers, you will know all about the impact that regular Bible reading has on your faith and the value of daily notes to guide, inform and inspire you.

Here are some recent comments from *New Daylight* readers:

'Thank you for all the many inspiring writings that help so much when things are tough.'

'Just right for me – I learned a lot!'

'We looked forward to each day's message as we pondered each passage and comment.'

If you have similarly positive things to say about *New Daylight*, would you be willing to share your experience with others? Could you ask for a brief slot during church notices or write a short piece for your church magazine or website? Do you belong to groups, formal or informal, where you could share your experience of using Bible reading notes and encourage others to try them?

It doesn't need to be complicated or nerve-wracking: just answering these three questions in what you say or write will get your message across:

- How do Bible reading notes help you grow in your faith?
- Where, when and how do you use them?
- What would you say to people who don't already use them?

We can supply further information if you need it and would love to hear about it if you do give a talk or write an article.

For more information:

- Email **enquiries@brf.org.uk**
- Telephone +44 (0)1865 319700, Monday to Friday 9.30 am–5.00 pm
- Write to us at BRF, 15 The Chambers, Vineyard, Abingdon OX14 3FE

Enabling all ages to grow in faith

At BRF, we long for people of all ages to grow in faith and understanding of the Bible. That's what all our work as a charity is about.

- Our **Living Faith** range of resources helps Christians go deeper in their understanding of scripture, in prayer and in their walk with God. Our conferences and events bring people together to share this journey, while our Holy Habits initiative helps whole congregations grow together as disciples of Jesus, living out and sharing their faith.

- We also want to make it easier for local churches to engage effectively in ministry and mission – by helping them bring new families into a growing relationship with God through **Messy Church** or by supporting churches as they nurture the spiritual life of older people through **Anna Chaplaincy**.

- Our **Parenting for Faith** team coaches parents and others to raise God-connected children and teens, and enables churches to fully support them.

Do you share our vision?

Though a significant proportion of BRF's funding is generated through our charitable activities, we are dependent on the generous support of individuals, churches and charitable trusts.

If you share our vision, would you help us to enable even more people of all ages to grow in faith? Your prayers and financial support are vital for the work that we do. You could:

- Support BRF's ministry with a regular donation;
- Support us with a one-off gift;
- Consider leaving a gift to BRF in your will;
- Encourage your church to support BRF as part of your church's giving to home mission – perhaps focusing on a specific ministry or programme;
- Most important of all, support BRF with your prayers.

Donate at **brf.org.uk/donate** or use the form on pages 143–44.

One size fits all?

For just as the body is one and has many members, and all the members of the body, though many, are one body, so it is with Christ. For in one Spirit we were all baptised into one body.

1 CORINTHIANS 12:12 (ESV)

Trying to make something that works for everyone is an immensely difficult task – ask anyone who has ever tried to plan a group holiday! Throw that out to the entire world – we know that people are wonderfully and remarkably different and we change so much throughout our lives as well. From babies to children to adults to older people, everyone is spectacularly unique.

Our mission as a charity is to encourage all people of all ages to grow in their faith. We share the message of God's love for the world in many different ways, because we know that a one-size-fits-all approach doesn't work with the profoundly varied world our God created.

From our Living Faith team creating Bible reading notes for individuals, like the ones you are holding now, to our Parenting for Faith team working to empower parents to raise God-connected children and teenagers. From our Messy Church team resourcing and equipping leaders to run church that reaches out to families to our Anna Chaplaincy team sustaining those working with older people, combatting loneliness and bringing comfort.

We're always looking for new ways to help people grow in faith as well as ways to reach more people with the things we do. Our work is only possible because of generous donations from individuals, charitable trusts and gifts in wills. If you would like to help us make what we do possible through a regular gift, find out how to give at **brf.org.uk/friends** or get in touch with our fundraising team on 01235 462305 or via **giving@brf.org.uk**.

Your prayers, as ever, are hugely appreciated.

Judith Moore
Fundraising development officer

Give. Pray. Get involved.
brf.org.uk

Please note our new subscription rates, current until 30 April 2023:

Individual subscriptions
covering 3 issues for under 5 copies, payable in advance
(including postage & packing):

	UK	Europe	Rest of world
New Daylight	£18.30	£26.25	£30.15
New Daylight 3-year subscription (9 issues) (not available for Deluxe)	£53.55	N/A	N/A
New Daylight Deluxe per set of 3 issues p.a.	£22.50	£32.85	£38.85

Group subscriptions
covering 3 issues for 5 copies or more, sent to one UK address (post free):

New Daylight	£14.55 per set of 3 issues p.a.
New Daylight Deluxe	£18.00 per set of 3 issues p.a.

Please note that the annual billing period for group subscriptions runs from 1 May to 30 April.

Overseas group subscription rates
Available on request. Please email **enquiries@brf.org.uk**

Copies may also be obtained from Christian bookshops:

New Daylight	£4.85 per copy
New Daylight Deluxe	£6.00 per copy

> All our Bible reading notes can be ordered online
> by visiting **brfonline.org.uk/subscriptions**
>
> *New Daylight* is also available as an
> app for Android, iPhone and iPad
> **brfonline.org.uk/apps**

NEW DAYLIGHT INDIVIDUAL SUBSCRIPTION FORM

All our Bible reading notes can be ordered online by visiting
brfonline.org.uk/subscriptions

Title .... First name/initials .... Surname ....

Address ....

.... Postcode ....

Telephone .... Email ....

Please send *New Daylight* beginning with the September 2022 / January 2023 /
May 2023 issue (*delete as appropriate*):

(*please tick box*)	UK	Europe	Rest of world
New Daylight 1-year subscription	☐ £18.30	☐ £26.25	☐ £30.15
New Daylight 3-year subscription	☐ £53.55	N/A	N/A
New Daylight Deluxe	☐ £22.50	☐ £32.85	☐ £38.85

Optional donation to support the work of BRF £ ....

Total enclosed £ .... (cheques should be made payable to 'BRF')

Please complete and return the Gift Aid declaration on page 143 to make your
donation even more valuable to us.

Please charge my MasterCard / Visa with £ ....

Card no. ☐☐☐☐ ☐☐☐☐ ☐☐☐☐ ☐☐☐☐

Expires end ☐☐ ☐☐   Security code ☐☐☐   Last 3 digits on the reverse of the card

To set up a Direct Debit, please complete the Direct Debit instruction on page 159.

We will use your personal data to process this order. From time to time we may send you
information about the work of BRF. Please contact us if you wish to discuss your mailing
preferences **brf.org.uk/privacy**

Please return this form with the appropriate payment to:
BRF, 15 The Chambers, Vineyard, Abingdon OX14 3FE
For terms and cancellation information, please visit **brfonline.org.uk/terms**.

Bible Reading Fellowship is a charity (233280) and company limited by guarantee (301324),
registered in England and Wales

ND0222

NEW DAYLIGHT GIFT SUBSCRIPTION FORM

☐ I would like to give a gift subscription (please provide both names and addresses):

Title _____ First name/initials _____ Surname _____

Address _____

_____ Postcode _____

Telephone _____ Email _____

Gift subscription name _____

Gift subscription address _____

_____ Postcode _____

Gift message (20 words max. or include your own gift card):

_____

_____

Please send *New Daylight* beginning with the September 2022 / January 2023 / May 2023 issue (*delete as appropriate*):

(*please tick box*)

	UK	Europe	Rest of world
New Daylight 1-year subscription	☐ £18.30	☐ £26.25	☐ £30.15
New Daylight 3-year subscription	☐ £53.55	N/A	N/A
New Daylight Deluxe	☐ £22.50	☐ £32.85	☐ £38.85

Optional donation to support the work of BRF £ _____

Total enclosed £ _____ (cheques should be made payable to 'BRF')

Please complete and return the Gift Aid declaration on page 143 to make your donation even more valuable to us.

Please charge my MasterCard / Visa with £ _____

Card no. ☐☐☐☐ ☐☐☐☐ ☐☐☐☐ ☐☐☐☐

Expires end ☐☐☐☐   Security code ☐☐☐   Last 3 digits on the reverse of the card

To set up a Direct Debit, please complete the Direct Debit instruction on page 159.

Please return this form with the appropriate payment to:
BRF, 15 The Chambers, Vineyard, Abingdon OX14 3FE
For terms and cancellation information, please visit **brfonline.org.uk/terms**.

Bible Reading Fellowship is a charity (233280) and company limited by guarantee (301324), registered in England and Wales

You can pay for your annual subscription to our Bible reading notes using Direct Debit. You need only give your bank details once, and the payment is made automatically every year until you cancel it. If you would like to pay by Direct Debit, please use the form opposite, entering your BRF account number under 'Reference number'.

You are fully covered by the Direct Debit Guarantee:

The Direct Debit Guarantee

- This Guarantee is offered by all banks and building societies that accept instructions to pay Direct Debits.

- If there are any changes to the amount, date or frequency of your Direct Debit, Bible Reading Fellowship will notify you 10 working days in advance of your account being debited or as otherwise agreed. If you request Bible Reading Fellowship to collect a payment, confirmation of the amount and date will be given to you at the time of the request.

- If an error is made in the payment of your Direct Debit, by Bible Reading Fellowship or your bank or building society, you are entitled to a full and immediate refund of the amount paid from your bank or building society.

- If you receive a refund you are not entitled to, you must pay it back when Bible Reading Fellowship asks you to.

- You can cancel a Direct Debit at any time by simply contacting your bank or building society. Written confirmation may be required. Please also notify us.

Instruction to your bank or building society to pay by Direct Debit

Please fill in the whole form using a ballpoint pen and return with order form to:
BRF, 15 The Chambers, Vineyard, Abingdon OX14 3FE

Service User Number: | 5 | 5 | 8 | 2 | 2 | 9 |

Name and full postal address of your bank or building society

To: The Manager	Bank/Building Society
Address	
	Postcode

Name(s) of account holder(s)

Branch sort code

☐☐ - ☐☐ - ☐☐

Bank/Building Society account number

☐☐☐☐☐☐☐☐

Reference number

☐☐☐☐☐☐

Instruction to your Bank/Building Society
Please pay Bible Reading Fellowship Direct Debits from the account detailed in this instruction, subject to the safeguards assured by the Direct Debit Guarantee. I understand that this instruction may remain with Bible Reading Fellowship and, if so, details will be passed electronically to my bank/building society.

Signature(s)

Banks and Building Societies may not accept Direct Debit instructions for some types of account.

Enabling all ages to grow in faith

Anna Chaplaincy
Living Faith
Messy Church
Parenting for Faith

100 years of BRF

2022 is BRF's 100th anniversary! Look out for details of our special new centenary resources, a beautiful centenary rose and an online thanksgiving service that we hope you'll attend. This centenary year we're focusing on sharing the story of BRF, the story of the Bible – and we hope you'll share your stories of faith with us too.

Find out more at **brf.org.uk/centenary**.

To find out more about our work, visit
brf.org.uk

Sharing
the Story
since 1922